Currency Areas

Also by John R. Presley

European Monetary Integration
(with Peter Coffey)

Currency Areas
Theory and Practice

John R. Presley
and
Geoffrey E. J. Dennis

Macmillan of Canada/Maclean-Hunter Press

First published 1976 by
THE MACMILLAN PRESS LTD
London and Basingstoke

First published in North America 1976 by
THE MACMILLAN COMPANY
OF CANADA LIMITED
70 Bond Street
Toronto M5B 1X3

ISBN 0-7705-1452-9

Printed in Great Britain

For my mother and father

For Penny

Contents

Preface

The idea for the book grew from a dissatisfaction over the wide gulf between the theoretical approaches to currency areas and the actual movement within the EEC towards European Monetary Union. In this book, we have been inspired by the work of a great many writers including R. A. Mundell, H. G. Johnson, R. I. McKinnon, P. B. Kenen, J. M. Fleming and G. Magnifico. In addition, the work of many others too numerous to mention has helped us formulate our ideas. The footnotes adequately reflect the acknowledgements that are due.

Both authors have received advice from several quarters. Thanks are due to Professor Swann for his encouragement and comments upon our work on currency areas, and to other colleagues at Loughborough University, particularly Tom Weyman-Jones. Thanks are also due to the staff seminar groups in the Economics Departments at the universities of Loughborough and Durham for some helpful comments and suggestions on earlier work. We would also like to thank Graham Smith of the University of Manchester for computing advice in some of the empirical work.

The typing of the manuscript was quickly and efficiently carried out by Joyce Tuson and Gloria Brentnall. They both deserve the highest praise for their ability in deciphering the authors' illegible hand.

Finally, Barbara and Penny deserve thanks for their patience and encouragement during the production of the book. Geoffrey Dennis would like to thank his wife Penny for typing an earlier draft and commenting on it simultaneously. In addition, John Presley would like to thank Catherine, Joanne and Katie. The patter of tiny, and not so tiny, feet is a welcome sound to a struggling author!

All these people are absolved from blame for any inaccuracies that may remain, the responsibility for which is the authors' alone.

J. R. P.
G. E. J. D.

A*

Introduction

This study has been stimulated by the attempts from 1969 onwards to create an Economic and Monetary Union in the European Economic Community by 1980. The theoretical survey of Chapter 2, and the empiricism of Chapter 3, represent an assessment of the feasibility of introducing a currency area in the Community, where a currency area is defined as either a common currency area or an area within which totally fixed exchange rates operate.

As a preliminary to this study, it is important to realise what Economic and Monetary Union might entail in the EEC, and how far the EEC has already progressed towards such a union.

ECONOMIC AND MONETARY UNION: A DEFINITION

The Werner Report,[1] perhaps the most authoritative document that has yet appeared from the Community, defines monetary union as having:

> inside its boundaries the total and irreversible convertibility of currencies, the elimination of margins of fluctuation in exchange rates, the irrevocable fixing of parity rates and the complete liberation of capital movements.[2]

This can be achieved either by maintaining national currencies or by establishing a single Community currency. Technically, the choice between these two possibilities is immaterial, but from a political and psychological viewpoint a single currency is favoured, as it would confirm the irreversibility of the venture.

The features of an economic union relate, not to currencies and to foreign exchange markets, but to fiscal and monetary policies. Economic union in the EEC would have two main characteristics – economic co-ordination and economic harmonisation. The former, in very simple terms, means that initially there might be community-level consultations concerning the drawing up of national budgets and national monetary policies. This would involve Community recommendations on the size of each of the main items of national budgets, on the appropriate variations in public spending and taxation, and in the methods of financing budget imbalances. Later on, if the Werner Report is to be believed, the power over economic policies would be transferred to the Community:

. . . monetary union implies the following principal consequences:
. . . the creation of liquidity throughout the area and monetary and credit policy will be centralised.
. . . monetary policy in relation to the outside world will be within the jurisdiction of the Community.
. . . the essential features of the whole of public budgets, and in particular variations in their volume, the size of balances, and the methods of financing or utilizing them, will be decided at the Community level.[3]

The second main characteristic of an economic union is that it has within its boundaries economic harmonisation. This, it is hoped, will remove all barriers that exist preventing the free mobility not only of labour, but also of capital and of entrepreneurship. Harmonisation is an attempt to remove any diverse practices in the economic field amongst member states. If successful, it will bring about similarities in tax structures, and to some extent tax levels (notably in relation to value added taxation, excise duties, the tax treatment of interest, and company taxation). In the monetary field it will produce similar instruments of monetary policy in each member state, and identical interest rate levels.

THE PROGRESS TOWARDS MONETARY UNION SINCE 1969
The wealth of plans put forward since the first Barre Plan of February 1969 gives a false impression of the progress made so far in establishing a monetary union. In many ways the volume of plans simply reflects a disagreement between

member countries as to how monetary union should come about. Thus, the initial plans, for example the Second Barre and Schiller Plans presented in February 1970, were representative of the two schools of thought on union, the 'monetarist' and the 'economist'. The later plans, in particular the Second Werner Report, were no more than compromises attempting to bridge the gap between the two schools of thought.

The main distinction between the two approaches to monetary union lies in the ordering of events in the process of monetary union. The 'monetarists', led by France, favour a swift imposition of fixed exchange rates and strict controls on capital mobility within the EEC, to be followed by economic co-ordination and harmonisation. In contrast, the 'economists', led by West Germany, emphasise the virtues of introducing economic co-ordination and free capital mobility before exchange rate rigidity is contemplated. Economic co-ordination is here taken to mean the introduction of closer co-operation and consultation between member states in the determination of economic policy objectives and policy action; this must be distinguished from harmonisation, which as suggested earlier is the imposition of similar fiscal systems within each member state. This clash of opinion has obviously influenced what the Community has set out to achieve, and in fact has achieved, since the early initiative towards union was taken in 1969.

Progress, or lack of it, towards monetary union can be recognised in several different areas, in particular in relation to the balance of payments, currency support, and exchange rate adjustment.

The Balance of Payments and Exchange Rates

As early as February 1970 a system was introduced for providing financial aid to those member countries experiencing balance of payments and currency difficulties. This support took the form of authorising the central banks of the original six member countries to provide automatic and unconditional credit to the extent of $1000m. to any member country in need of such facilities. The French and West German central banks were each to provide $300m.,

Italy was to provide $200m., with Belgium–Luxembourg and the Netherlands each providing $100m. It is important to note that these credits were loans bearing an interest charge for periods of between three to six months, not gifts of currency. A further $1000m. worth of short-term credits was to be made available, if necessary, with similar contributions from each country, but this further credit was to be conditional upon the borrowing country accepting Community guidance, perhaps on its future balance of payments policy. As regards medium-term credits, the European Commission proposed the introduction of $2000m. worth of such credits, the duration of loans being from two to five years, with the same breakdown of contributions as for short-term credits. The management of medium-term aid rests with the Council of Ministers which decides the duration and interest charged on any medium-term loan.

To reconcile the conflict between 'monetarists' and 'economists' on the question of exchange rates, the Committee of Governors of the central banks, within the framework of the second Werner Committee, put forward a proposal which appeared at that time to be ingenious. This so-called 'snake in the tunnel' mechanism to bring about a gradual reduction in exchange rate margins has, since it was first introduced, met with a number of setbacks.

Before the dollar crisis in August 1971 each currency was allowed to fluctuate to a level 1 per cent either side of its par value with the dollar; thus, there was a 2 per cent 'band' of fluctuation (the difference between the upper and lower limits of possible fluctuation in value of a currency against the dollar). As the par value of each currency was determined only against the dollar, this meant that the cross rate of any two EEC currencies could fluctuate by up to 4 per cent. This would occur, for example, when one of the currencies moved from its lower limit against the dollar to its upper limit, whilst the other currency moved from its upper limit to its lower limit against the dollar. To prevent such wide movements in exchange rates the governors of the central banks suggested that the 'band' of fluctuation against the dollar should remain at 2 per cent over time, but at any point in time the extent by which EEC currencies would be allowed to fluctuate against each other was to be reduced to 2·4 per cent. This was to be achieved by fixing each month, by agreement between the member countries, a 'Community level' for the dollar between the band of 2 per cent, but not necessarily mid-way between the upper and lower limits of the band. At any point in time the value of any EEC currency was to be maintained within a range 0·6 per cent either side of the community level of the dollar; although over a period of time the value of any currency could fluctuate by 1 per cent either side of the dollar parity (through movements in the community level of the dollar). If, for example, currency *B* is at the lower limit in relation to the dollar, currency *A* would not be allowed to go beyond a level 1·2 per cent greater than the lower limit. This effectively reduces the potential range of variation of intracommunity exchange rates.

The dollar problem of 1971 prevented the introduction of such a system. However, the agreement of March 1972 called for the start, initially on an experimental basis, of a very similar exchange rate system before 1 July 1972. (In fact, this was introduced on 24 April 1972). The principal differences between this agreement and the previous proposal lie in the percentages that are employed in relation to exchange rate margins. Since the dollar crisis the band against the dollar has been increased to 4·5 per cent; thus, the tunnel has grown wider. Each member agreed to keep its currency at any point in time within approximately 1·12 per cent either side of the currency level for the dollar, compared with the original proposal of ·6 per cent.

Even this has proved difficult to operate. Britain, Ireland and Italy are still operating outside the Community snake, and France have only recently returned the franc to the snake. Clearly the Marjolin Report's conclusion that in relation to monetary union the EEC has moved backwards since 1969 is fully justified.

Co-ordination and Harmonisation

Progress in relation to economic co-ordination has also been disappointing in the light of what the Werner Report proposed. Closer co-operation and consultation between member countries in formulating economic objectives, and in particular, demand management policies to attain these objectives, was called for and was to be achieved in a number of ways. The Council of Ministers was to set medium-term objectives for Community members and to work out programmes to attain them. This was to be aided by tri-annual surveys of the economic climate within the Community. The first was to examine the previous year's performance and to revise objectives if necessary. The second was to review current policy and to lay down guidelines for policy in the following year, even to the extent of establishing preliminary budgets for member countries. The final survey would work out the guidelines in more detail as regards national budgets and make sure that all national budgets were compatible. It was hoped that, in addition, a number of Community economic indicators could be established which would provide warnings against impending economic dangers. In practice this has not fully materialised as yet.

The Council of Ministers does meet three times each year to examine the economic climate in the Community, and it does put forward very general policy objective guidelines; but there is no detailed attempt to formulate economic policy, as the Werner Report envisaged, to achieve these objectives. Co-ordination Committees have been set up, their main function being to monitor the national policies and to examine them in relation to the common guidelines laid down by the Council. Even the European Commission, however, admits that little progress has been made in co-ordination: 'few concrete measures have been adopted beyond recommendations of a very general nature.'[4]

Limited tax harmonisation has been brought about by the use of the value added tax throughout the Community: but even in relation to VAT important differences persist between states as regards both the definition of the tax assessment basis and the rates charged. There are plans to harmonise taxes on subsidiaries, mergers, investments and dividends, and excise duties. The delay in implementing these plans has been due, according to the European Commission, to the accession of the new member states.

Wide divergencies do exist on the relative reliance of member states on direct and indirect taxation. For example, France takes only 17 per cent of its total taxation in the form of direct taxes, 43 per cent in the form of indirect taxation, and the remainder from social security contributions. Contrast this with the case of Britain where 43 per cent is gathered from direct taxation, 39 per cent from indirect, and 17 per cent from social security contributions.[5] Clearly a lot remains to be done in relation to harmonisation.

It is against this background that our study takes place. Our objective is to use that economic theory which relates to currency areas, and an empirical study based upon it, to examine the economic suitability of the EEC for a currency area, and to indicate the possible economic repercussions resulting from a currency area should it be introduced.

2 A Survey of Currency Area Theory

Economic theory unfortunately does not fit into very easily defined compartments. It would be convenient to argue that the only relevant part of theory, as far as monetary integration in Europe is concerned, is that which has been labelled 'optimal currency area' theory; but this is not true. One only needs to examine the possible stages in the movement towards a common currency in Western Europe to appreciate that theory alone cannot provide all the answers. A common currency cannot be introduced instantaneously. Monetary integration may exhibit a number of possible stages; there may be a move initially towards a fixed exchange rate system, and this might be accompanied by various degrees of centralisation in the decision making process. Whether or not monetary and fiscal policies show total, partial, or no supranational control in a currency area will determine the effectiveness of integration and the ability of the participants to achieve economic objectives; for this reason it is worthwhile in this chapter to go outside the theory of optimal currency areas to examine the operation of so called policy-mixes under a fixed exchange rate regime. (A currency area is defined as an area over which exchange rates are totally fixed or a common currency exists.)

Not only might there be changes in relation to policy weapons, but policy targets may change in the integration process. A collective agreement on economic objectives may be a possible feature of this; eventually integration may be carried to such an extent that there is a redefinition of the balance of payments at the currency area level away from the national level. It may no longer be necessary for member states to maintain payments' equilibria, provided the currency area as a whole is in equilibrium. Applied to the EEC, this would undoubtedly require political unification and a willingness on the part of surplus countries to subsidise those in deficit. All the possible twists and turns in the movement towards a currency area make a thorough theoretical study very difficult, if not impossible, to accomplish. Theory is often limited by the fact that it proceeds under the assumption that the introduction of a currency area means no more than the adoption of a common currency in that area, or the maintenance of fixed exchange rates within that area. In reality it may mean much more than this.

The pioneering work on currency areas and fixed exchange rate unions was that of Meade and Scitovsky.[1] Theory has attempted to remain at least one step ahead of the process of economic integration in Europe. The article by Meade, for example, examined amongst other issues the consequences of an integration of financial arrangements in Europe upon the achievement of payments equilibrium. Many of the features which have since appeared in official documents in the EEC were discussed including the effects of supranational controls on economic policy, centralised regional policies, and single currency and banking systems. In fact, Meade came to the conclusion that a common currency offered perhaps the best long-run solution to the achievement of payments equilibria in the EEC. The first contribution to the theory of optimal currency areas as such was that of Mundell,[2] which in turn gave rise to important contributions from McKinnon[3] and Kenen.[4] This can be viewed as a branch of the fixed versus flexible exchange rate debate. A currency area with a common currency and a flexible external exchange rate may be more advantageous than either a worldwide fixed or flexible exchange rate system.

The term 'optimal' is somewhat vague and misleading in the latter group of theories. It appears to refer to an ideal or perfect position as it would do in welfare theory, the objective being the maximisation of the achievement of price stability, full employment, and payments equilibrium. Mundell defines optimality 'in terms of ability to stabilise national employment and price levels'.[5] He proceeds to define an economic region as an optimal currency area when it exhibits characteristics which lead to an automatic removal of unemployment, and payments' disequilibria; automatic in the sense that no interference is required from monetary and fiscal policies to restore equilibria. This approach is repeated by both Kenen and McKinnon. Little or no mention is made of the possible advantages which might arise from the replacement of several currencies by a single currency within a region. Attention is focused instead upon those characteristics which tend to minimise the disadvantages which might arise in a currency area in the form of internal and external disequilibria. The conclusion given is that a currency area should be formed in that economic region where such costs can be minimised, the implication being that the maximum net benefits of a currency area would then be accomplished. Optimal currency area theory therefore concentrates upon defining those characteristics which yield cost minimisation. It is in relation to differences in suggested characteristics that theories can be distinguished from one another.

The question posed in these theories is different from that of later work on currency areas and exchange rate unions by Fleming[6], Magnifico[7] and Wood[8], amongst others. Mundell seeks to define the perfect economic region for a currency area. The result is that the formation of an optimal currency area would involve a redefinition of frontiers in that the area may not conform to national boundaries. It would be determined by the localisation and concentration of industries rather than by political, linguistic or sociological factors. This is clearly a less realistic approach than that which seeks to determine whether or not a given group of countries should form a currency area or an exchange rate union, but it does, nevertheless, provide a basis for empirical study of the EEC, as will be seen later.

A common fault of much of the literature[9] is to assume that a totally rigid exchange rate system, involving perhaps a multitude of currencies, yields exactly the same advantages and disadvantages as a single currency area. Johnson[10] and Mundell[11] argue to the contrary. In some respects the two regimes are similar. It is often suggested that both would reduce the risks of destabilising currency speculation by eliminating completely the possibility of exchange rate adjustment within the area. Both would lower the probability of a breakdown of the international monetary system and a return to barter and bilateral trading. If the balance of payments continues to be defined at the national rather than the currency area level, both systems would impose a discipline upon government policy to restore internal and external equilibria in the absence of automatic adjustment. This would not exist to the same degree under a more flexible exchange rate system. However, a fixed exchange rate system would not diminish to the same extent the costs of valuation and conversion of different currencies that a single currency would. It would still necessitate the provision of financial services involved in converting currencies. Too many currencies within an area would lower the usefulness of money as a medium of exchange and as a store of value. The extreme position would exist where the number of currencies exceeded the number of tradable commodities. Here a barter system would be more efficient than the monetary mechanism. A fixed exchange rate regime may still allow hidden barriers to the freedom of competition within a customs union in the form of currency restrictions. These would be more difficult to impose given a single currency. In addition, a common currency seems more permanent than the simple locking of exchange rates. As far as the EEC is concerned, a fixed exchange rate system would be seen by most 'Europeans' as a poor substitute for a common currency in that it would not produce the same encouragement to the process of political unification, the transfer of power to the Community level over, for example, monetary and fiscal domains, and it would not provide the same challenge to the US dollar in the international monetary system that a single currency might bring about. It is important to bear such distinctions in mind in what follows.

Theories relating to currency areas and exchange rate unions have a tendency to fall into either of two categories. The first is what will be called the 'automatic adjustment' theory. This type of theory seeks to determine the characteristics of a currency area which will bring about the automatic achievement of internal and external balance without government interference. The second type is a more policy-orientated approach. It attempts to establish the necessary economic environment where monetary and fiscal policies can be totally relied upon to create equilibria in the absence of exchange rate adjustments; that is, it recognises government interference in the economy whereas the former does not.

This chapter lays the foundations for an empirical study of the feasibility of a currency area in the EEC. It begins with a survey of the theories of optimal currency areas, an examination of the characteristics by which the optimality of a region is defined, beginning with the factor mobility thesis of Mundell, followed by McKinnon's emphasis on the proportion of tradable goods, and ending with an examination of Kenen's stress on product diversification. This is followed by a survey of the more recent attempts to determine the factors influencing the effectiveness of economic policies within exchange rate unions. The chapter ends with a discussion of the monetarist view of the formation of a currency area.

FACTOR MOBILITY

Assume that a currency area consists of two countries, *A* and *B*. Each country wishes to maintain both internal and external balance, that is, full employment and payments equilibrium. Initially, equilibria exist in each country. If *B*'s demand for *A*'s exports now declines, *A* will have a payments' deficit and unemployment, *B* will have a payments' surplus and over-full-employment given that there is an attempt in *B* to substitute domestic production for *A*'s exports. In the absence of exchange rate adjustment, disequilibria would necessitate deflation in *A* and reflation in *B*. Should *B* introduce a tight monetary policy, the burden of adjustment would fall mainly on *A*. Higher unemployment would be required to reduce the demand for imports in *A*, to divert production to exports, and to stabilise if not reduce prices, making the trading position more favourable. It is precisely to avoid the necessity for this kind of adjustment that movements in exchange rates have been advocated as an alternative to sacrifices in employment. A devaluation of *A*'s currency would restore external balance by making imports more expensive and exports relatively cheap, given that import and export demands are sufficiently elastic.

Exchange rate adjustment, however, would not be necessary to correct disequilibria where factor mobility exists between *A* and *B*. An optimal currency area, according to Mundell, is that region which exhibits high internal factor mobility and low external factor mobility: 'If the world can be divided into regions within each of which there is factor mobility and between which there is factor immobility, then each of these regions should have a separate currency which fluctuates relative to all other currencies.'[12]

How might factor mobility work in our example? The fall in demand for *A*'s exports would lead, through multiplier effects, to a decline in the employment of labour and capital in *A*; in *B* the demand for factors of production would be increasing. Hence labour and capital would flow from *A* to *B*. The unemployment problem is cured in *A* through an outward flow of labour and capital. The switch to the consumption of domestic production in *B* away from imports would again, through the multiplier process, stimulate increased income in *B*, which would raise imports from *A*. The immigrants into *B*, earning income, would swell the purchase of imports from *A*; at the same time *A* has a lower earning-population and therefore its imports from *B* would decline. *A*'s deficit is reduced, as is *B*'s surplus. Internal and external balance are restored.

Mundell constructed his theory on the assumption that differential unit factor costs between countries would cause the initial disturbance to payments' equilibria. Such differential movements could be prevented if factors flow in response to differentials. Factors should ideally flow to high cost areas away from low cost areas, thus avoiding the occurrence of competitive imbalance between areas; in this manner payments problems arising through divergent cost–price increases between members of a currency area are prevented and the currency area can be considered as optimal. Labour flows are seen as a substitute for exchange rate adjustment, which itself is seen as a substitute for changing real wage levels as a consequence of changing demand and supply conditions.

This argument falls down when it is appreciated that differential changes in unit factor costs are not the only possible causes of disequilibria, as may have been the case in our example. Secondly, even if it is conceded, for example, that the original external imbalance was caused by higher unit labour costs in *A* and hence higher export prices, factors may not flow from *A* to *B*. Higher unit labour costs may reflect higher real wages in *A*, depending upon the relative levels of labour productivity in *A* and *B*. Labour may not be prepared to move from high wage areas to low wage areas, even if more jobs are available in low wage areas. Instead it may be content to wait until jobs become available in *A*; even if labour and capital are prepared to flow from *A* to *B* they may still set up forces which do not lead to the restoration of equilibria. The flow of factors to *B* from *A* will tend to reduce the rate of increase in unit factor costs in *B* by increasing the supply of factors; whilst in *A* the supply of factors is diminished and the rate of change in unit factor costs increased. This tends to worsen *A*'s competitive position *vis-à-vis* *B*; thus, the reduction of unemployment through mobility is at the expense, in this case, of external equilibria. The movement of factors in any case from *A* to *B* would be against that predicted by Mundell since *A* is the high unit factor cost area. Labour may, indeed, be tempted to move from *B* to *A*, provided it can find employment where unemployment already exists. This might help restore payments equilibria, but it would certainly be at the expense of employment. Either way it may be impossible to produce both internal and external balance through mobility.

It does not automatically follow that factors will flow from low unit factor cost areas to high factor cost areas. This was hinted at in the last paragraph. Factors of production are attracted to move by the rewards for their services offered in different areas. It does not necessarily follow that high unit cost areas are also high wage areas. It may simply mean that output per man is so low in the high cost area that, even with lower real wages there than elsewhere, unit labour costs are higher; that is, the ratio of wages to productivity, which determines unit labour cost may differ between areas.[13] If labour is attracted by the real wage level one might find in this case that labour flows in the opposite direction, from high unit cost to low unit cost areas. This again would tend to exaggerate the competitive imbalance between the two areas. The adjustment process is further complicated in practice by the inflexibility of wages and prices in a downwards direction, and by the influence of trade unions upon wage levels. This would interfere with the free market mechanism seen in Mundell's theory.

The limitations to the success of factor mobility in securing equilibria in our example do not end here. Given the factor flow from *A* to *B*, external disequilibria would be exaggerated if industry in *B* is experiencing increasing returns to scale. The increased availability of factors in *B* would lower unit costs and dampen price rises; whilst in *A* a reduction in the scale of production may increase unit costs and, in turn, prices.

Secondly, the increased demand for factors in *B*, as a consequence of the increase in domestic demand, may not be sufficient to absorb the unemployed factors in *A*, which arise from the decline in its exports and the subsequent multiplier effects. This will depend upon the nature of the relative production functions in the expanding industries in *B*, and the declining industries in *A*; that is, upon their respective employment of labour and capital. If, for example, the expanding industries in *B* are capital intensive, and the declining industries in *A* are labour intensive, the net result may be a continuance of labour unemployment in *A*, and capital shortage in *B*. Wage inflexibility in *A* would mean that unemployment without government interference would persist.

A further complication arises once it is recognised that all units of a factor are not identical. Different units of labour have different skills and abilities. One would suspect that the more mobile units of labour are also the younger, and perhaps more productive, elements of the labour force. If this is so, mobility in the long run may produce disturbances to the competitive relationship between countries.

It has been assumed that an increase in demand in *B* creates an increase in the demand for capital in *B*, and a flow of capital from *A* to *B*. International capital flows, however, are not geared entirely to changes in the demand for capital. The flow will be determined partly by the anticipated rate of return on capital, and the risks of investing in another country as well as the level of economic activity. The increased demand for capital in *B* does not necessarily imply that the rate of return on capital is higher than in *A*, nor that investment is less risky there. In so far as investors have specific views over time of the riskiness of investment in certain areas, this is likely to interfere with the free flow of capital in response to disequilibria. The response of capital flows to disequilibria is crucially important, since capital is needed to finance investment, and investment in turn determines employment through the multiplier process.[14]

The arguments above have been put forward as part of a static approach. The movement of factors from one country to another takes time. Although it is convenient for the economist to assume *ceteris paribus,* in practice other things do not remain constant. Industrial organisation and technology are continually changing. By the time factors have changed location it may be necessary for the flow to occur in the reverse direction to counteract disequilibrating forces. The example chosen in this section is but one of several possible situations which might arise in relation to internal and external disequilibria between two countries. What would happen, for example, if *A* and *B* were both subject to unemployment at the same time, perhaps caused by a loss of export demand as a result of a world recession? How could factor mobility provide an equilibrating mechanism in this case?

More fundamental than this long list of complications which cast doubt on our original example, is the proposition that factor mobility should not be encouraged anyway. This has been the basis of regional policy in a number of countries, including the United Kingdom. Work has been encouraged to move to the workers rather than vice versa. The justification for this policy is partly to be found in the under-utilisation of social capital which labour mobility creates in the depressed areas of the economy, and the over-utilisation and shortage in the prosperous regions. In addition, one may find damaging repercussions on the social and economic environment in the depressed areas. Factor movements tend to persist in certain directions for a long period, rather than being reversed frequently as predicted by the adjustment mechanism outlined here. Growth would be centred in particular areas, and regional problems would be enlarged, not diminished.

Heckscher and Ohlin[15] suggest that factor prices will be equalised between countries through trading without factor mobility, although this has received critical comment. Clearly, to meet Mundell's criterion for optimality, currency areas would need to be geographically small for sufficient mobility to be obtained, but not too small to dismiss the advantages of a monetary economy. This may involve establishing currency areas within existing countries, rather than advising a group of countries to form a currency area.

Since this discussion was stimulated by Mundell's contribution to the optimal currency area debate, it seems fitting to let Mundell have the final comment upon it: 'A currency area . . . cannot prevent both unemployment and inflation among its members.'[16]

Factor mobility does not, therefore, provide all the answers in yielding both internal and external balance in a currency area.

THE OPENNESS OF THE ECONOMY

McKinnon's theory proposes that currency areas should comprise highly open economies. His view of optimality is very similar to that of Mundell. The optimality of a currency area is defined in relation to its ability to achieve internal and external balance:

> Optimum is used here to describe a single currency area within which monetary fiscal policy and flexible external exchange rates can be used to give the best resolution of three (sometimes conflicting) objectives: (a) the maintenance of full employment; (b) the maintenance of balanced international payments; (c) the maintenance of a stable internal average price level.[17]

A currency area should be imposed in so far as it minimises the cost of achieving these objectives, with particular stress, in contrast to Mundell's emphasis on payments equilibrium (for reasons explained later), upon internal price stability. There is little reference in McKinnon's original article to the possible benefits that might accrue in a currency area, other than with respect to the above cost minimisation.

The characteristic which determines whether or not a currency area should be formed is the 'ratio of tradable to non-tradable goods'. A tradable good can be either an exportable or importable good. Exportables are those goods produced domestically which are either consumed domestically or exported. Hence, they will exceed exports by the extent to which domestic consumption takes place from potential export production. Importables are produced and consumed domestically as well as being imported. Non-tradables are goods which, principally through the exclusive costs of transportation across national frontiers, do not enter into trade. The higher is the ratio of tradables to non-tradables the more beneficial will be the formation of a currency area.

Comparing this criteria with that put forward by Mundell, it would appear realistic to argue that the greater is the volume of trade between members of a currency area, the more mobile will factors of production be; but it must nevertheless be recognised that factor mobility is determined by other influences: for example, by the degree of homogeneity of labour and by the existence of political and sociological barriers to mobility.

The crucial argument in the McKinnon thesis is that the higher is the percentage contribution of importable and exportable goods to total domestic consumption, the greater will be the impact of an exchange rate adjustment upon the domestic price level. When all domestically consumed goods are either exportables or importables, for example, a devaluation of 10 per cent will raise the domestic price level by 10 per cent.

The desired effects of devaluation would be to correct a trade deficit, to stimulate increased domestic production of exportables and importables, and to diminish domestic consumption. Exports can then be increased and imports reduced. This desired effect may only be accomplished through an increase in the domestic price level; the greater the ratio of tradable to non-tradable goods the greater the disturbance to the price level and the more valid the case against flexible exchange rates. Secondly, such an exchange rate policy may reach its goal of external equilibria only if there is sufficient domestic unemployment to allow increased production of tradable goods.

The more open is an economy the less effective will flexible exchange rates be in curing a trade imbalance, and the more damaging will that flexibility be to domestic price stability. As the domestic prices of tradable goods move with the exchange rate, the higher is the proportion of tradable goods in the economy the less is the possibility that adjustments to domestic consumption can take place to alter export and import flows; the more also will the general price level be affected, since tradable goods' prices take an increasing weight in the determination of the domestic price index.

The achievement of internal price stability is regarded as the key economic objective. Price instability does not allow money to effectively fulfil its functions as a store of value, unit of account, or medium of exchange; it is seen as an impairment to the growth of income and of trade, and a discouragement to specialisation. It also induces domestic capital to be transferred into other currencies. Mundell saw the equalisation of unit factor costs being important in the adjustment process; but this might involve variations in price levels. Internal price stability is emphasised much more in the McKinnon thesis. Open economies, according to McKinnon, should rely upon monetary and fiscal policies not exchange rate variations, to control trade flows. When a trade deficit exists only a relatively small reduction in spending will be necessary to bring adjustment when the economy is open. As exportables and importables are a large part of total spending, a relatively small reduction in demand, for example, would be sufficient to release exportables from domestic consumption, and to reduce imports, thus improving the trade balance. In a closed economy a much greater deflationary policy would be required to yield the necessary adjustment. This would be more damaging to domestic employment. Hence, the greater the ratio of tradable to non-tradable goods the smaller is the required reduction or increase in spending to maintain external balance. This can be demonstrated by a simple numerical example:

	Open economy	*Closed economy*
Marginal propensity to import (MPM) $= \dfrac{\Delta M}{\Delta Y}$	0·8	0·1
External deficit	£80m.	£80m.
Change in income to correct deficit	$\Delta Y = \dfrac{\Delta M}{0 \cdot 8}$ $= £100\text{m.}$	$\Delta Y = \dfrac{\Delta M}{0 \cdot 1}$ $= £800\text{m.}$

This disturbance to employment therefore would be much greater in the closed economy case. The reduction in spending in the latter example is felt mainly in the non-tradable goods sector. On the export side also, in an open economy there will be a high propensity to consume exportables. A relatively small reduction in demand would be sufficient to divert exportables away from domestic consumption compared with that required in a more closed economy. Not only would employment not suffer unduly from the use of monetary and fiscal policies in an open economy, but also price stability could be promoted much more than under a flexible exchange rate. If excess demand exists in an open economy it will be shown not in an increase in prices, but in an increased demand for imports, much more than in a closed economy. Excess demand can be eliminated through domestic restrictive policies. Such policies would, in an open economy, simply reduce imports and restore external balance, without damaging employment. In a closed economy excess demand leads to wage and price rises which can only be controlled through deflationary policy at the expense of employment.[18]

This theory is not strictly an automatic adjustment theory. Nevertheless, it does argue that the more open is the economy the more advantageous is a currency area, and the less is the degree to which monetary and fiscal policies need to be used to maintain equilibria.

An additional justification that open economies should form currency areas is to be found in relation to the existence of money illusion. Mundell argues that:

> The thesis of those who favour flexible exchange rates is that the community in question is not willing to accept variations in its real income through adjustments in its money wage rate or price level, but that it is willing to accept virtually the same changes through variations in the rate of exchange . . . Now as the currency area grows smaller and the proportion of imports in total consumption grows, this assumption becomes increasingly unlikely.[19]

This really anticipates McKinnon's theory. The last sentence in the quotation supports the importance of the ratio of tradable to non-tradable goods in determining the success of a currency area. The classical case for flexible exchange rates is based upon the proposition that changes in domestic price and wage levels are necessary to restore external balance. Such changes may not be obtainable through domestic policy, since real wages may be inflexible in a downwards direction. This inflexibility has been blamed partly upon trade unions' reluctance to accept a decline in living standards for their members. Exchange rate movements, however, might be successful in changing real wages and restoring external equilibria. Trade unions may not recognise that a devaluation, for example, leads to an increase in the cost of living and a reduction in real wages. The more open an economy becomes however, that is the larger the proportion of trade that takes place, the more unlikely it becomes that this kind of money illusion will persist. As more trade occurs, the greater will be the effect of devaluation on the domestic price level, and the more certain it will be that trade unions recognise the decline in living standards and real wages which results; their reaction must be to prevent this decline, which in turn limits the effectiveness of exchange rate movements.

This theory of optimal currency areas rests on two beliefs. The more open is an economy, the greater is the efficacy of economic policy designed to cure external disequilibria, and the less effective is exchange rate depreciation in bringing a lower real wage and restoring equilibria.

Beginning with domestic full employment and price stability, and assuming external disequilibria, the theory does yield satisfactory methods for the restoration of external balance; but it does fail in its policy recommendations when internal disequilibria arise. If initially unemployment occurs in a very open economy through, for example, technological change affecting the capital intensiveness of industries, it becomes difficult to get rid of this unemployment through monetary and fiscal policies without disturbing the external balance. An expansionary policy would be seen primarily in an increase in imports with little impact on unemployment. In this case it may be advantageous to devalue. Expansionary policy would have more effect on curing unemployment in a closed economy than it would in an open economy. A small change in spending would be required in a closed economy to eliminate unemployment, and there would be a less detrimental effect on the payments' position.

Secondly, McKinnon makes an implicit assumption that the world price of tradable goods is constant. In the present economic climate this assumption is not valid. A relaxation of this assumption would again lead to a challenge of his theory. External disequilibria may be caused, for example, by an increase in world prices. With a fixed exchange rate this increase in world prices would be communicated to the domestic price level. In a totally open economy a 10 per cent rise in world tradable goods prices would bring a 10 per cent rise in the domestic price level with fixed exchange rates operating. The more open the economy the greater would be the impact of changing world prices on the domestic price level, given a currency area. Price stability, the major objective in McKinnon's theory, would be impossible to obtain. The totally opposite conclusion would be justifiable here. More open economies should have flexible exchange rates to protect them from changes in world prices. There have been a number of occasions recently where this can be seen in evidence. In Western Germany, for example, higher inflation rates in other countries have been communicated, given fixed exchange rates, through higher import prices to domestic prices. It was partly to avoid this that Germany floated its currency in 1971.

Whether or not flexible or fixed exchange rates are to be advocated in an open economy to maintain internal price stability depends therefore upon the source of the disturbances to external equilibria. If it is caused by an external demand change fixed exchange rates can be the order of the day. If it is, for example, caused by differential rates of inflation in trading countries, which may be the result of varying cost-push pressures, a more feasible solution would be exchange rate variation to insulate the internal price level.[20]

The adjustment mechanism outlined earlier assumes that a high ratio of tradable goods to non-tradable goods, or a high average propensity to import, would reflect a high marginal propensity to import. It does not necessarily follow that is so. If any economy is at full employment a subsequent increase in demand may result in a rapid increase in imports, more so than if the economy had unemployed resources. There may be a high marginal propensity to import, even if the average propensity to import is low. Similarly if imports consist of luxury items, any increase in domestic income may have a significant effect on importation, even though overall the level of trade compared, for example, to gross national product is low. It does not, therefore, automatically hold that monetary and fiscal policies will be more effective in more open economies.

Taken to its logical conclusion, McKinnon's criteria for currency areas would involve the introduction of such an area at the world level; the world cannot have external disequilibria, and worldwide monetary and fiscal policies can be relied upon to yield internal, world objectives.

PRODUCT DIVERSIFICATION

The third major contribution to optimal currency area theory is that of P. B. Kenen. In this is found yet another possible characteristic which will give optimality in the sense defined by Mundell: the determination of the suitability of introducing a currency area is related to the 'diversity in a nation's product mix, the number of single product regions contained in a single country'.[21]

Kenen makes three claims; the first:

(1) a well diversified national economy will not have to undergo changes in its terms of trade as often as a single product national economy.[22]

The more diversified is an economy, particularly in relation to exports, the more independent it will be of foreign disturbances; that is, there will be a smaller repercussion upon the payments position, and upon domestic price and income stability than there would be in a less diversified economy, as a result of foreign disturbances. The basis of this argument is the belief that positive changes with respect to some exports will be offset by negative changes with respect to others; as demand for some increases, the demand for others falls. The more diversified are export products, the greater will be this offsetting mechanism. When a country relies upon a small number of exports, equilibrium will be very sensitive to changes in the prices and demands for these goods. No offsetting mechanism will operate. The less diversified economies may need flexibility in exchange rates, the more diversified will not. This conclusion is supported by Kenen's second and third claims:

(2) when . . . it [a diversified economy] does confront a drop in the demand for its principal exports, unemployment will not rise as sharply as it would in a less-diversified national economy.

(3) links between external and domestic demand, especially the link between exports and investment, will be weaker in diversified national economies, so that variations in domestic employment 'imported from abroad will not be greatly aggravated by corresponding variations in capital formation'.[23]

If, for example, changes in export demand are to cancel each other out in a diversified economy, this will only have a neutral effect on employment if labour is mobile between occupations. A decline in export demand for textiles, for example, may be offset by an increase in demand for some other export, but the employment level can only be maintained if textile workers can find employment elsewhere, perhaps in the expanding export industry. This argument suffers from one of the defects recognised in Mundell's theory. It does not necessarily arise that capital–labour ratios are equal in expanding and declining industries; if not, there is forced to be unemployment of either labour or capital through even changes in export demand which totally offset one another.

Similarly, in relation to price and wage changes, export demand changes may not be neutral in a well diversified economy. Where the demand for export products increases there will probably be increases in prices and wages within those sectors; where demand falls it is unlikely that wages and prices will also fall, perhaps again because of trade union reluctance to allow them to do so. In fact, if trade unions are particularly strong they may be able to gain wage increases on the basis of comparability with wage increases in the expanding sectors. Overall, therefore, prices and wages may not remain constant but increase.

Kenen himself realised the major limitations of his theory. Foreign disturbances are not always offsetting. Changes in export demand often occur in the same direction as a consequence of cyclical movements in other economies. Such changes are interdependent not independent. Equilibria under fixed exchange rates or a common currency are not cushioned from the impact of disturbances by some averaging process.

The McKinnon and Kenen approaches to optimality are incompatible. McKinnon advocates that more open economies should maintain internal fixed exchange rates, and external exchange rate flexibility. Yet if the more open economies join together they become more diversified. On Kenen's criterion they should then maintain fixed, not flexible exchange rates. Secondly, a country which produces a small range of products may indulge in heavy external trade. In one theory it merits fixed exchange rates, in another flexible rates. At the other extreme one would suspect that more diversified economies rely less upon trade than less diversified economies. If this is so the two theories again lead to opposing recommendations.

COST–BENEFIT ANALYSIS
One of the major drawbacks to the studies outlined above is

their failure to sufficiently emphasise the benefits of a currency area which might arise other than in relation to achieving equilibria. Some of these benefits were hinted at earlier in the discussion of the similarities and differences between common currency areas and exchange rate unions. This deficiency is not to be found in Wood's analysis of a currency area.[24] Wood treats the question of the feasibility of a currency area not as an optimality problem, but as a cost–benefit question. A monetary union should be introduced if the benefits from union outweigh the costs. In applying this analysis to the EEC, five potential benefits are listed and quantified. There are gains from resource saving, mainly in the realm of banking and foreign exchange dealing. Gains arise from resource reallocation; in Wood's study these result from the pooling of reserves which may take place in a currency area. There are the gains from increased trade and reduced uncertainty which are a common feature of the literature supporting fixed versus flexible exchange rates. Finally there are the gains from a more efficient working of the monetary mechanism mentioned earlier. The potential cost, which might arise through the inability to alter the exchange rate to correct imbalances, has to be set against these benefits. This has already been discussed and will be emphasised again in the last section of this chapter.

THE POLICY-MIX APPROACH

Optimal currency area theory represents a search for those characteristics which make for an efficient attainment of internal and external balance. Mundell sought factor mobility which would bring about automatic adjustment. McKinnon and Kenen sought those features of a currency area which, although not yielding automatic adjustment, would promote only a minimal use of monetary and fiscal policy with fixed exchange rates. A third approach is that which argues that monetary and fiscal policies can be relied upon to give equilibria whatever the characteristics of the currency area. It is not strictly part of optimal currency area theory, in that it does not lay down rules for optimality – but is obviously relevant in considering the EEC. This can be labelled the policy-mix approach.

The effectiveness of monetary and fiscal policies under fixed exchange rates is determined partly by the definition of external balance. Initially external balance will be taken to mean current account balance as opposed to overall balance, which introduces the capital account. Given this initial definition of equilibrium, domestic policy designed to influence capital flows has no relevance for the attainment of equilibrium and can be excluded from the range of expenditure-switching policies available to a government.

Such a definition of external balance introduces a potential conflict between internal and external equilibrium when total responsibility for their achievement is placed on monetary and fiscal policies. This can be illustrated by taking a Keynesian view of policy, and ignoring the possible price effects of economic policy. Expenditure reducing policies (deflationary) will act upon excess-demand inflation; expenditure increasing policies will counteract unemployment. Variations in spending, however, will also influence trade. Increased spending will generate more imports, the change depending upon the marginal propensity to import, and may divert exports to the domestic market. Reduced spending will have the opposite effects. With these influences operating, in some situations there is no apparent conflict in attaining internal and external balance by expenditure changes. Over-full employment, that is inflation, and a payments deficit can be remedied by deflationary policy. Expansionary policy can be successful where unemployment and a payments surplus exist. A difficulty arises in that the expenditure change required to restore internal balance may not be the same as that necessary for external balance.

The conflict is more obvious where inflation exists alongside a payments surplus, or where unemployment exists alongside a deficit. In both events, the expenditure change necessary to bring internal adjustment conflicts with that required for external adjustment. Deflationary policy aimed at curing inflation will worsen the payments surplus. Expansionary policy to cure unemployment worsens the payments deficit.

All is not lost if external balance is redefined and one recognises possible differential effects of monetary and fiscal policies.[25] If one can accept that external equilibrium means more than a current account balance, that is, that it implies an overall balance on current account plus certain capital items, then theoretically monetary and fiscal policies may still be able to give full equilibrium through their effects on capital flows. Expansionary domestic policies, by increasing income, will increase saving and therefore the funds available for foreign investment. The natural result would be a worsening of the balance of payments, through an increased capital outflow. This effect is counteracted by the greater optimism generated by expansionary policy. Project expectations may improve, diverting foreign investment to the domestic economy and attracting capital from abroad. The net effect of income changes in the capital account will depend upon the relative strength of the two opposing pulls. The impact of expansionary fiscal policy on the balance of payments will be different from that of expansionary monetary policy, despite these similar effects on the capital account through income changes. There are a number of reasons why this differential impact may occur. Expansionary fiscal policy will lead to further inflows of capital than those generated by greater optimism on the part of businessmen. Keynesians would argue that given a fixed money supply and no change in the velocity of circulation of money, an increase in income through fiscal means will raise the rate of interest by lowering the money supply available for speculative purposes (outside the liquidity trap region). The rise in interest rates will attract foreign capital. Secondly, such policy must take the form of either increases in government expenditure or tax reductions. The nature of these fiscal changes may be such that again foreign capital is attracted, by increasing the rate of return on capital. A specific example of this would be the lowering of profits taxation. These arguments suggest that expansionary fiscal policy will have a favourable effect on the capital account. The opposite conclusion can be reached in the case of expansionary monetary policy. McKinnon and Oates [26] and R. Mundell[27] have doubted the wisdom of monetary policy designed to influence domestic equilibrium. They conclude that under a system of fixed exchange rates, with free movement of financial assets between countries, monetary policy cannot alter the level of income in the economy. This negates the effects of income changes on the capital account brought about by monetary policy simply by dismissing the ability of monetary policy to change income. On the other hand, expansionary monetary policy, increasing the money supply, will lower the rate of interest, leading to a capital outflow. This type of policy therefore worsens the capital account balance. Given these differential effects of monetary and fiscal policies on the capital account, it is possible to derive the appropriate 'policy-mix' which will cope with the conflict situations outlined earlier. A balance of payment deficit (wider meaning) and unemployment could be eliminated by deflationary monetary policy combined with expansionary fiscal policy. A balance of payments surplus and over-full employment would necessitate deflationary fiscal policy and an expansionary monetary policy. There still appears, theoretically, to be some 'hope' for a fixed exchange rate system.

Eventually the problem of securing external balance may disappear at the national level where the formation of a currency area is accompanied by political unification. In this situation the balance of payments may be redefined at the currency area and not the national level. Deficit regions may then be financed by surplus regions. At the 'national' level internal adjustment would be emphasised. More reliance may be placed on regional policy, particularly if fiscal and monetary harmonisation is a feature of the currency area. Internal adjustment policies, decided at a supranational level however, would still need to take account of their effects upon the currency areas' external balance. One of the main dangers inherent in the 'monetarist'[28] approach to monetary union in the EEC is the desire to achieve fiscal and monetary harmonisation before the balance of payments is defined at the Community level. The introduction of similar rates and types of taxes, for example, throughout the Community is a major restriction on the flexibility of fiscal policy to alleviate imbalances.[29]

The subject of 'policy-mixes' deserves a book in itself; here are only the bare bones of the approach. To enter into a comprehensive survey of its limitations would involve a thorough examination of all the writings on monetary and fiscal policies, the theoretical structures and empirical evidence on which their operations are based. This the reader must find elsewhere.[30]

Let it be sufficient to say that there are two main limitations to the analysis; first, internal and external balance are not the only economic objectives of modern governments. Monetary and fiscal policies have functions to perform in relation to achieving economic growth, redistributing income and wealth, and reallocating resources. Policy designed for internal and external balance may conflict with the attainment of these other objectives. Growth, for example, may be damaged by stop–go policies for economic stability and trade balance. One is reminded of Tinbergen's conclusion[31] that in order to achieve n policy objectives, there are required at least n types of policy action. Secondly, internal balance does not lend itself to a simple definition. In most economies there is a trade-off between inflation and employment. It is on this trade-off that the final section of this chapter concentrates.

THE PROPENSITY TO INFLATION

Economists actively began discussing the feasibility of several countries forming a currency area in terms of the 'Phillips' Curve'[32] in 1971. Fleming argued, 'At least as important as any of the factors so far discussed . . . is the extent to which costs in the various parts of the fixed exchange rate area tend to rise at similar or at different speeds when employment is at nationally acceptable levels.'[33] Magnifico suggested that countries with similar national propensities to inflation should form currency areas,[34] and even Coffey and Presley observed that:

> General agreement on the required level of unemployment may produce different rates of inflation between countries because of the differing nature of the Phillips' Curve from country to country. Alternatively the acceptable rate of inflation may be accomplished at the expense of varying levels of unemployment between countries, and varying welfare costs.[35]

The Phillips' Curve traditionally indicates the impossibility of achieving full employment and wage rate stability simultaneously. Wage rate rises in excess of productivity rises lead to price increases, hence the incompatibility between low unemployment and low inflation rates. The simple concept of internal balance that has been assumed so far is invalidated.

FIGURE 2.1

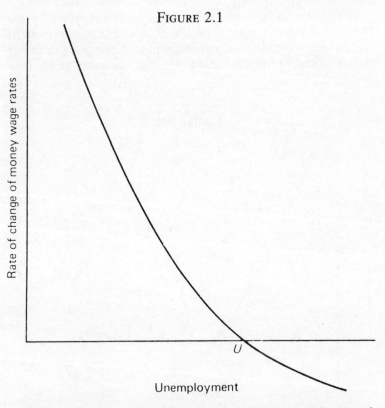

Figure 2.1 depicts the relation between rates of change of money wage rates and levels of unemployment as shown in Phillips' evidence. The lower the level of unemployment, the greater will be the demand for labour, and the higher will be the rate of change of money wage rates. At a level of unemployment (U) the rate of change in money wage rates will be zero. Stress is laid upon the relation between the rate of

change of *money* wage rates, not *real* wage rates, *nor* prices, and the level of unemployment. However, one can reinterpret the curve in terms of an inflation–unemployment trade-off, given that the rate of change of money wage rates is the key determinant of price changes, and that the rate of increase in productivity is known. The rate of change in productivity is important as it can neutralise the effect of an increase in money wage rates on unit labour costs.[36]

The trade-off between inflation and unemployment presents governments with a policy choice. Each government will have a preference at any point in time for one particular inflation–unemployment point on the trade-off curve (see Figure 2.2).

FIGURE 2.2

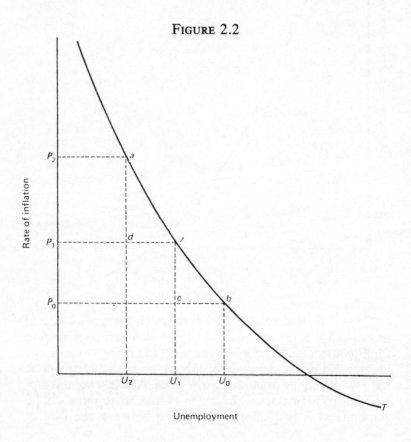

Unemployment

The preference point will be determined with reference to the country's payments position, and the sacrifice, in terms in unemployment, which has to be made to restrict inflation to a specific level. A reduction in the rate of wage inflation increases the level of unemployment.

Whether or not countries should form a currency area is answered by an examination of respective inflation–unemployment trade-offs. Magnifico introduces the concept of the national propensity to inflation. This propensity is a function of the trade-off existing in a country and the government's view of the desirable rate of price change. If national propensities to inflation differ between countries; the formation of a currency area is not feasible since the consequential differences in inflation rates would bring payments difficulties which would need to be corrected by exchange rate adjustment.

Consider the case of two countries, A and B (Figure 2.2) each having the same inflation–unemployment trade-off (T). Country A has a preference for point a and B for point b on the trade-off. If they form a currency area, given substantial trade between the two countries, A will be subjected to a trade deficit with B. Exchange rate adjustment would be required unless A, on forming the currency area, is willing to deflate, increasing unemployment from U_2 to U_0, or B is prepared to inflate, reducing unemployment from U_0 to U_2, or unless both are prepared to compromise by agreeing upon an acceptable rate of inflation (e.g. P_1). Despite a possible compromise A still needs to make a sacrifice in employment $(U_2 - U_1)$, although overall the inflation–unemployment trade-off for the currency area improves. If, for example, $cb = dz$ then the average level of unemployment in the currency area will remain the same:

$$\frac{U_2 + U_0}{2} = U_1$$

but the average rate of inflation will decline, if the trade-off is steeper between az than zb, hence:

$$ad > zc \quad \text{and} \quad \frac{P_2 + P_0}{2} > P_1$$

An improvement in the trade-off is not a reflection that both countries are subjected to welfare gains in excess of losses. Country A may view the reduction in inflation as inadequate compensation for the increase in unemployment. What is required on forming a currency area, therefore, is not only a similarity in trade-off between countries but also identical preference points on that trade-off curve.

This conclusion can be enlarged upon by considering the case where trade-offs differ. In Figure 2.3 A and B now have trade-offs T_1 and T_2, respectively. Assume that the initial preference points on this transformation function are a and b. As before, the formation of a currency area without any previous agreement on a common inflation rate will lead B into deficit, and a consequent need for deflationary policy in B and inflationary policy in A. If the creation of a currency area brings with it a common inflation rate objective P_0, A will have a higher inflation rate and B a higher level of unemployment.

What is evident from Figure 2.3 is that A and B in operating as a currency area must be subject to widely different levels of unemployment (U_1 and U_2) at the target rate of inflation of P_0. In addition if the trade-off in B is more elastic (T_3) the common inflation rate adopted may involve severe sacrifices in employment there, clearly a heavy cost of a currency area. There is little hope of achieving a common agreement on an employment objective in such a monetary union. A defined employment objective U_0, for example, would lead to rapid inflation in B (P_2) compared with A (P_1). In a currency area where a large volume of intra-area trade exists, it is unlikely that a common employment objective will be established. Much more emphasis will be placed on achieving external balance by reaching a defined price rise target. Since this prevents payments difficulties and presumably reduces the possibility of an international transmission of cyclical movements through trade variations. The only situation where there may be less emphasis on agreeing a common inflation rate is where the balance of payments is defined at the currency area level. In this case, the joint inflationary experience of A and B will need to be determined such that there is no detrimental effect on their combined external balance. This does not necessarily mean that each country needs to subject itself to the same inflation rate.

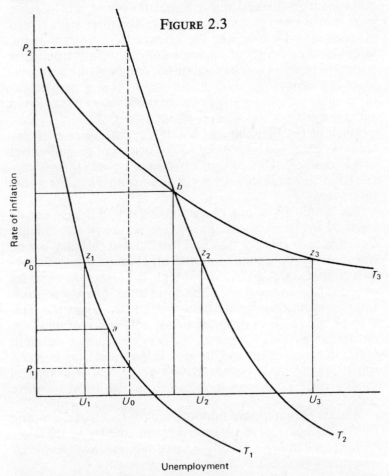

FIGURE 2.3

The choice of the common inflation rate (i.e. agreement on the position P_0 above) is itself a complex one. Sumner states, 'since inflation imposes unambiguous costs, there is no economic case for compromising on a target higher than the lowest national inflation rate currently prevailing, and a strong case for a target of zero.'[37] This is, however, a tall order and would result in an increase in unemployment in all member countries except the country (countries) which already exhibited the target rate of inflation. Although only 'minimal constraints' should be placed 'on the speed of adjustment',[38] the end result would represent considerable increases in unemployment for those countries with a high inflation rate. By choosing the average inflation rate as the target level, the costs of forcing countries to shift from their preferred position will be minimised. Although the desirability of low or zero inflation is undeniable, it may be preferable to approach this in stages due to the inability to prevent a simultaneous rise in unemployment.

Much of the Fleming and Magnifico analysis of currency areas is concerned with isolating the causes of dissimilarities in the trade-off. This, in turn, enables guidelines to be ascertained as to where countries are good candidates for a currency area.

The trade-offs of our two countries *A* and *B* may not be identical for two reasons. Firstly, the nature of the Phillips' Curve in each country may be identical, but this may not be transferable into a common trade-off because either productivity growth rates differ, for example through differing rates of technological progress, or because wage inflation acts differently on price inflation between the two countries. This may be the result of differences not only in factor markets, but in the markets for goods and services; that is, different forms of competition and, in turn, different pricing policies, might prevail. As a consequence a given rate of change of money wage rates may have a differential effect on price inflation.

What is perhaps more important is the fact that the nature of the Phillips' Curve varies from one country to the next. Three possible explanations of this dominate the literature,[39] Magnifico summarises these in this manner:

> Differences in the national propensity to inflation would seem to depend *inter alia* on historical and social factors, on the system of industrial relations and the militancy of trade unions, on the structure of industry and its regional deployment as well as on the building into the general public psychology of expectations of inflation or price stability generated by demand management policies.[40]

The first, following Hines[41] terminology, stems from trade union 'pushfulness' (measured by the rate of change of unionisation which is independent of the demand for goods and services and labour), differing between countries. Such differences could only be eliminated in a currency area by introducing a common system of industrial relations and collective bargaining. Secondly, the differing development and structure of industry between countries brings about unequal levels of frictional unemployment. Greater frictional unemployment would shift the Phillips' Curve to the right. The achievement of similar levels of frictional unemployment would necessitate currency-wide regional policies involving industry and worker relocation. Thirdly, anticipated inflation is not the same in all countries; as a result, the nature of the Phillips' Curve, according to Friedman and Phelps amongst others,[42] is continually changing. This latter explanation needs closer attention.

THE MONETARIST APPROACH
Friedman[43] maintains that there is a fallacy in the Phillips' Curve approach. Instead of measuring the rate of change of *money* wage rates on the vertical axis, the rate of change of *real* wage rates should be measured. This error in construction requires a new Phillips' Curve to be derived for each anticipated rate of growth of money wage rates (Figure 2.4).

The natural level of unemployment is defined by the point of intersection of that Phillips' Curve which assumes a zero anticipated rate of wage inflation with the horizontal axis (U_0). If the government attempts to keep unemployment at a level less than (U_0), for example at (U_1), the rate of change of money wage rates will be y. As a result people will revise their view of anticipated wage inflation above the original zero level, and the short-run Phillips' Curve will shift to the right and inflation will accelerate. This argument has led to the proposition that the long-run Phillips' Curve may in fact be vertical (PP), above the natural level of unemployment U_0. This would occur if inflation is fully anticipated, that is if money illusion does not exist.

If the long-run Phillips' Curve is vertical, the question of when countries should form a currency area needs to be reconsidered, since in the long run the level of unemployment will tend towards its natural level. The decision to form a currency area will be made in the light of the natural levels of unemployment which prevail in potential member countries. The lower are the natural rates, the lower will be the costs of attaining a common inflation rate, and therefore the more worthwhile the formation of a currency area will be. To this criticism of the original Phillips' Curve approach one can add the 'new' monetarist view on how to get rid of differing national propensities to inflation. Parkin writes, 'differential rates of domestic credit expansion are the cause of both exchange rate adjustments and differential rates of inflation.'[44]

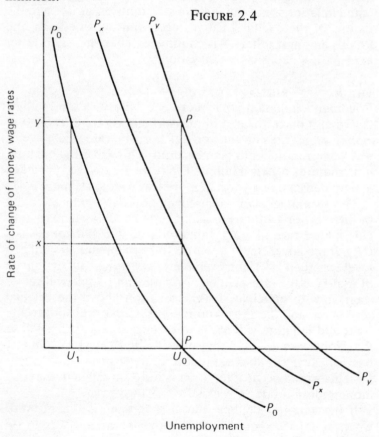

FIGURE 2.4

The solution is viewed as being straightforward. By equalising domestic credit expansion between member countries, inflation rates can similarly be equated. Payments disequilibria would no longer materialise; hence, there would be no need for exchange rate adjustment. There is no reference in Parkin's thesis to the differential costs in terms of unemployment which might be generated by such a policy.

A COMMON CRITICISM

The plea for an equalisation of inflation rates as a requisite for a currency area is a feature of most recent writings which adopt a Phillips' Curve–trade-off approach. Although such a view is appealing because of its simplicity, it may be ill-founded. It seems to imply that by equalisation, payments difficulties can be avoided. This is not so. The rate of change of the value of exports and imports is not only determined by the rate of change of their prices, but also by the rate of change of their demands. This latter factor is neglected in the recent debate. Countries differ in the composition of their trading partners. One must remember that equalising inflation rates within the currency area says nothing about what is happening to inflation rates in trading partners outside the area. Income and price elasticities of demand for exports and imports differ between countries,[45] even where inflation rates are identical.

The following simple numerical example over five time-periods will demonstrate the impact of such differences on trade. The following assumptions are made:

(i) There are only two countries in the model (A, B) trading with each other. Therefore any deficit incurred by one country is counterbalanced by a surplus in the other country.

(ii) In period 0, the two countries are in balance of payments equilibrium (i.e. imports = exports – with capital movements ignored).

(iii) The growth rate of GNP in A and B is 5 per cent per annum.

(iv) Inflation in A and B is running at 5 per cent.

(v) The import–GNP ratio in *A* and *B* is initially 0·1.

(vi) The relevant import elasticities are:

	A	*B*
Price elasticity	−0·5	−1·5
Income elasticity	+3·0	+1·0

Table 2.1 shows that although, as one would expect, the countries' national product and, in particular, price indexes are kept in step, country *A* suffers an increasing balance of payments deficit, which, by Period 5, is as large as 7·2 per cent of GNP, with country *B* having, of course, an equal surplus.

This has occurred because:

(i) The higher income elasticity of demand for imports of *A* (+3·0) means its growth in demand for imports is three times as high as that of *B* (elasticity = 1·0) for any given change in income.

(ii) The lower price elasticity of demand for imports of *A* (−0·5) means its fall in demand for imports is only one-third as great as that of *B* (elasticity = −1·5) for a given change in prices.

These two factors combined show that, holding all of the factors constant, *A* will tend to move into deficit and *B* into surplus. The relevance of this simple two-country exercise for the EEC is clear despite the extreme elasticity differentials used in the exercise. If these relevant elasticities differ considerably between EEC members, a policy of equalising inflation rates may only exacerbate balance of payments disequilibria, and must be replaced by a deliberate policy to have differential inflation rates in an attempt to move towards the elimination of payments imbalances. The question of the level of the various elasticities is, of course, an empirical matter which will be treated in the next chapter.

It is on this final point which this survey seeks to lay attention. The quest for identical propensities to inflation is not necessarily a desirable objective given, in particular, differing elasticities of demand for exports and imports, between countries. The formation of a currency area needs to be decided according to the ability of the currency area to work together to achieve these differential rates of inflation necessary to preserve dynamic payments equilibria in all member

TABLE 2.1

Country A

Time	Imports $[M]t$ m	Exports $[X]t$ m	Trade balance $(X\text{-}M)$ $[B]t$ m	GNP $[GNP]t$ m	Price index $[P]t$ $t_0 = 100$
0 (Initial position)	100	100	0	1000	100
1 {Income effect	+15	+5			
Price effect	−2·5	−7·5			
Total	112·5	97·5	−15	1050	105
2 {Income effect	+16·875	+4·875			
Price effect	−2·813	−7·313			
Total	126·563	95·063	−31·5	1102·5	110·25
3 {Income effect	+18·984	+4·753			
Price effect	−3·164	−7·130			
Total	142·383	92·686	−49·697	1157·625	115·763
4 {Income effect	+21·357	+4·634			
Price effect	−3·560	−6·951			
Total	160·180	90·369	−69·811	1215·506	121·551
5 {Income effect	+24·027	+4·518			
Price effect	−4·005	−6·778			
Total	180·202	88·109	−92·093	1276·282	127·628

TABLE 2.1 (*continued*)

Country B

Time	Imports [M]*t* m	Exports [X]*t* tr	Trade balance (X-M) [B]*t* m	GNP [GNP]*t* m	Price index [P]*t* $t_0 = 100$
0 (Initial position)	100	100	0	1000	100
1 { Income effect	+5	+15			
Price effect	−7·5	−2·5			
Total	97·5	112·5	+15	1050	105
2 { Income effect	+4·875	+16·875			
Price effect	−7·313	−2·813			
Total	95·063	126·563	+31·5	1102·5	110·25
3 { Income effect	+4·753	+18·984			
Price effect	−7·130	−3·164			
Total	92·686	142·383	+49·697	1157·625	115·763
4 { Income effect	+4·634	+21·357			
Price effect	−6·951	−3·560			
Total	90·369	160·180	+69·811	1215·506	121·551
5 { Income effect	+4·518	+24·027			
Price effect	−6·778	−4·005			
Total	88·109	180·202	+92·093	1276·282	127·628

states, at the same time restricting unemployment to acceptable levels, or, if the monetarist approach is valid, to sufficiently small levels of natural unemployment as to make the currency area worthwhile.

APPENDIX: INTERNAL AND EXTERNAL BALANCE UNDER FIXED EXCHANGE RATES: A KEYNESIAN APPROACH

The interaction of monetary and fiscal policies in the attainment of internal and external balance can be illustrated using *IS/LM* curve analysis:

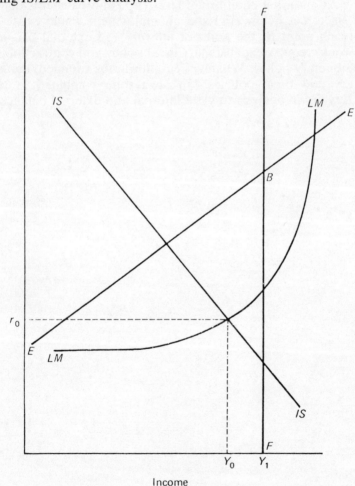

The line *EE* shows combinations of *r* and *Y* which give external balance. It slopes upwards because as income rises more importation takes place; this has to be counteracted by an increase in the rate of interest to attract an inflow of capital if external balance is to be maintained. *FF* is the line of internal balance, with full employment at Y_1.

A change in fiscal policy will bring a change in the *IS* curve; a change in monetary policy will lead to a change in the *LM* curve (except in the liquidity trap region).

At an initial equilibrium level (r_0, Y_0) a payments deficit (since it is below *EE*) and unemployment would exist. To reach point *B*, the point of internal and external balance, would require expansionary fiscal policy and contractionary monetary policy. Whatever equilibrium is assumed, monetary and fiscal policies can always be combined in this Keynesian analysis to yield internal and external balance.

3 Currency Areas Theory and the EEC

The various theories suggesting criteria for the optimal size of a currency area surveyed in the last chapter present the starting point for an analysis of the European Economic Community in this light.

In this chapter the evidence and conclusions on the optimality of the EEC as a currency area will be presented in such a way that it is of little consequence whether a full monetary union is set up in the EEC – with a common currency – or whether exchange rates amongst existing EEC currencies are simply locked together irrevocably, which is often depicted as being a less complete commitment to monetary union. A 'pseudo' union of this type is clearly much easier to opt out of by means of an exchange rate change than is a full union where, by definition, exchange rates cease to exist. This largely political question involving the permanence of a union is therefore not considered in the evidence to follow.

There are basically four main sets of reasons for the establishment of a monetary union in Europe. The first of these revolves around the social and political argument that a commitment to EMU would be a symbol of unity. However, as a step, perhaps the final one, towards economic unity, the existence of a monetary union is not simply desired on this idealistic ground. It is also often assumed that EMU is a crucial stage in the movement towards the ultimate goal of many advocates of the 'European ideal', political unity.

Secondly, and very important in practice, is the desire to establish an internationally acceptable currency as a counterweight to the American dollar. This has been particularly relevant since the late 1960s, when the Vietnam War was a major factor triggering off a period of considerable instability in the confidence in the dollar. The importation into the EEC of US inflation due to the use of the dollar as a vehicle or reserve currency up to 1971, and the vast flows of Eurodollars which came into existence as a result of the US balance of payments deficit of this time, have led to an often expressed wish that a European Currency should exist which could be floated or adjusted against the dollar. It is doubtful, however, if such a European currency would quickly achieve this replacement of the dollar. For the negotiations towards EMU have been a chapter of disputes on the relative movements of various EEC currency exchange rates, and it is therefore debatable whether agreement on common action *vis-à-vis* the dollar is very likely in the near future. Also deliberate action by the IMF to supplement the role of the dollar as a reserve currency by a European alternative would be needed, while it will take many years before the increasingly important multinational corporations cease to use the dollar for their transactions.[1]

It is also envisaged by some economists that a European currency could be set up to rival the dollar, while still maintaining individual member currencies whose exchange rates could be altered against this European currency. On this argument, a currency as a counterweight against the dollar is not sufficient for monetary union at all.[2]

Thirdly, a favourite argument for EMU is that it is necessary to ensure the success of the Common Agricultural Policy (CAP). It is widely believed that the stability of agricultural prices – a vital part of the CAP – will be attained in a fixed exchange rate environment. However, Johnson[3] has been one of many to point out that if there are differential rates of price and cost inflation in member countries, overall stability of any commodity prices is attainable only by appropriate exchange rate changes. Clearly, this argument is only valid if domestic cost and price trends can be kept in line.

A final set of arguments for EMU are the purely economic ones. A common currency is typically expected to yield advantages in terms of removing some uncertainty in trans-

actions between member countries, by extending the area
over which one currency acts as a medium of exchange and a
store of value and through the establishment of free factor
and goods movement which will augment the gains from
trade. Ironically, these forceful, traditional arguments in
favour of a common currency have not featured highly in the
debate on EMU. It would not be heretical to say that many
of the arguments which have been put forward have been
political and non-economic in character. It is the aim of this
chapter to change the emphasis somewhat and investigate
the economic case for monetary union in the EEC, in terms
of currency theory as it stands today.

In the evidence to follow, there will be less emphasis on
the 'automatic' adjustment theories of Mundell, McKinnon
and Kenen, due to their relative inappropriateness in a
world where government intervention in all economies is an
accepted thing. Concentration will be placed on the adjustment theories where the government has a role in influencing the choice between the twin targets of full employment
and low inflation.

FACTOR MOBILITY
Mundell[4] in the first major contribution to optimal currency
area theory concentrated on the need for factor mobility to
achieve internal balance.[5] He concluded that such mobility
can remove any need to resort to exchange rate changes. As
far as the two factors of production, labour and capital, are
concerned, their mobility in the EEC is a necessary criterion
for the establishment of a currency area that is optimal. Such
an area of perfect factor mobility is known in this theory as a
region.

As far as labour is concerned, the EEC clearly does not
correspond to a region. The EEC is too large, despite the
lower limit put on the size of a currency area by Mundell due
to the loss of 'moneyness' of a currency covering a very small
area. Meade[6] was perhaps the first to observe that labour
mobility in Western Europe (as compared to the UK)[7] was
low, causing him to recommend flexible rates between individual currencies as an alternative equilibrating solution.
The reason for this now widely accepted opinion is the exis-

tence of substantial barriers in terms of language and customs differences and also legal and professional constraints on labour mobility. Despite many attempts since the establishment of the EEC, little progress has been made in the removal of such 'man-made' barriers, while language and customs differences may never be completely removed. While such barriers exist, no substantial labour mobility is likely.[8]

There are perhaps two strands of hope from this discussion. First, Scitovsky[9] proposed the gradual establishment of a common currency believing that such a move in itself would generate small increases in labour mobility. However, this would have to be supplemented by a common labour market and employment policy for the whole Community. Boleat,[10] reiterating that language differences are most crucial, puts forward the view that the moves to harmonise such factors as social security payments, minimum wage laws and collective bargaining procedures are irrelevant, given these other far more critical problems. A counter-argument is that the reduction in price and cost differentials which should result from the introduction of a common currency will further reduce any incentive for labour to move from a low wage area to a high wage area. This is largely an empirical issue that cannot be resolved until a common currency is set up, but it is most unlikely that the resultant labour mobility will be able to replace exchange rate or real wage changes as a mechanism for attaining internal balance.

Secondly, as Corden has pointed out,[11] although intra-EEC labour mobility is low, the movement of labour from such countries as Greece, Turkey, Yugoslavia, etc. to areas of high labour demand such as West Germany and Northern Italy has helped to reduce the need for exchange rate changes. But this assumes that countries in deficit on the balance of payments will send foreign workers home in *large* numbers to alleviate their developing unemployment problem. This net migration from outside the Community will help alleviate disequilibrium problems but at the present time is in no position to replace high internal mobility as a stabilising policy.

For capital, the same indigenous language and cultural

barriers do not exist. The major restrictions on full capital mobility in the EEC are the regulations and controls placed on exchange markets in individual member countries. The liberalisation of capital movements has been a major objective of the EEC in recent years, and was a crucial element in the Werner Report, but little progress has been made to date. However, recent evidence had suggested that the major capital markets of Western Europe (i.e. Germany, France, Great Britain, Belgium and the Netherlands) have become increasingly well integrated.[12] This evidence is particularly interesting as the convergence in nominal interest rates in treasury bill and Eurodeposit markets in these countries is largely attributed to a convergence of inflation rates and exchange rate expectations.

Such evidence is encouraging to the proponents of EMU, but the delay in achieving a large degree of capital mobility during the history of the EEC is not difficult to account for. Firstly, in the currency upheavals of the early 1970s, any thoughts of increasing capital mobility were subsumed in often nationalistic responses to external events. It is much simpler to introduce controls to protect a currency in an unstable situation than it is to agree to remove such restrictions *ad infinitum*. Secondly, it has proved very difficult for individual countries in differing external payments positions to agree on common action in relation to the flows of dollars into Europe and other speculative 'hot money' movements. Thirdly, differences in individual members' institutions have led to no two assets being perfect substitutes, a fact which is not helped by there being no widely accepted risk-free Community asset. Such high substitutability of assets is an important element in an integrated capital market.

Nevertheless, the prospects for greater mobility of capital are much better than for labour. First, the establishment of a monetary union (particularly in the form of a common currency) should help to remove the resort to hastily erected exchange controls by individual countries. It was, perhaps, with this in mind that Scitovsky suggested that the establishment of a common currency would help capital mobility.[13] In addition, monetary union will increase the mobility of long-term capital flows by removing any uncertainty associated with individual currencies. Despite the stability of capital flows during the Canadian floating rates experiment of 1950–62, it is reasonable to suggest that the advent of fixed exchange rates or a common currency is likely to lead to more stability of capital flows than less stability.

Much of this recent volatility of capital has its origins in the large influx of dollars into Europe in recent years. Ironically, the response to these dollar flows – the development of the Eurodollar market – has increased substantially the degree of capital mobility in Europe.[14] The growth of capital mobility in Europe had been aided by the increasing importance of multinational corporations. These points suggest that the moves towards, and the establishment of, EMU should help to increase capital mobility considerably. The barriers to free mobility are man-made and there is no reason to believe that full monetary union will not be accompanied by a high degree of capital mobility.

OPENNESS

A second major contribution to currency area theory, by McKinnon,[15] put forward the view that the more 'open' an economy is, the greater the need for that economy to have fixed exchange rates to prevent any price instability caused as the exchange rate fluctuates. This argument has been criticised by Corden,[16] who states that if disturbances leading to price instability actually emanate from abroad, flexible rates will insulate the economy from such disturbances.[17] If this assumption is made, McKinnon's argument is turned on its head, with fixed rates being detrimental to a very 'open' economy. If, however, it can be assumed that the disturbances originate in the domestic economy, the McKinnon argument is entirely valid, and it is on this basis that an investigation of the EEC economies can be started.[18]

A major practical problem is the appropriate definition of openness. Numerous definitions have either been suggested or put into practice with the one used by McKinnon himself being 'the ratio of tradable to non-tradable goods'. Openness can also be defined in terms of the importance of 'tradables' and 'non-tradables' in the output or consumption of an economy. This dichotomy was used by Cross and Laidler[19] in the context of an inflation model for 'open' and 'closed' economies. The empirical problems of actually defining and measuring such aggregates are immense and, having failed to find an adequate empirical justification for the distinction in the UK equation, the authors did not consider the activity worth pursuing for other countries.[20] Another alternative lies in the much easier estimation of the Marginal Propensity to Import (MPM) and the measurement of the Average Propensity to Import (APM), with an 'open' economy expected to have relatively high values for these proportions. Balassa[21] dislikes the use of the APM as a measure of openness as imports are in value terms, while Gross National Product (GNP) is value-added and also includes non-traded goods. However, the inclusion of non-traded goods in no way invalidates the use of GNP as the denominator in a calculation of the APM – if such goods were excluded, the APM would clearly rise for all countries, without shedding any light on whether the degree of openness were any nearer to satisfying McKinnon's criterion. In addition, of course, the empirical problems of removing traded goods from any definition of GNP, as implied above when discussing 'tradables' and 'non-tradables', are immense. Balassa's alternative measures – the share of imports in the consumption of manufactured goods or the share of exports in manufacturing output – do not have the same empirical problems as using the traded *v*. non-traded goods distinction, but are not as comprehensive as the APM or MPM.

The Marginal Propensity to Import was estimated for all EEC members[22] by fitting the following equation:

$$M = a + b_1 Y \tag{1}$$

where M represents imports and Y Gross National Product and b_1 is the MPM.

In addition, the Average Propensity to Import was calculated as the import/GNP ratio:

$$\text{APM} = M/Y \tag{2}$$

Rather than simply taking the most recent APM as being

representative of the whole data span, the average of each annual figure was used, being the most satisfactory proportion to compare with the MPM estimated as it is from the period 1958–73:

$$\text{APM} = \frac{\sum\limits_{t=1}^{16} Mt}{\sum\limits_{t=1}^{16} Yt} = \frac{\sum\limits_{t=1}^{16} (M/Y)t}{n} \tag{3}$$

The results are reported in Table 3.1.

TABLE 3.1

	APM	MPM	$t(\text{APM}-b_1)$
Belgium–Luxembourg	0·388	0·558	2·3592
Denmark	0·276	0·263	0·3307
France	0·115	0·153	0·9844
Germany	0·145	0·160	0·4900
Ireland	0·366	0·389	0·4946
Italy	0·140	0·187	1·1179
Netherlands	0·394	0·402	0·2075
United Kingdom	0·172	0·236	1·3006

A resolution of the issue of whether the APM or MPM is more appropriate as an indicator of openness is perhaps more difficult. MPM only measures the incremental ratio of imports to income:

$$\text{MPM} = b_1 = \frac{dM}{dY} \tag{4}$$

while the APM, measuring as it does the total proportion of imports to GNP, is more comprehensive. The t statistics from a significance test comparing the values of the APM and MPM show that in practice there is no empirical difference between the two, except for Belgium–Luxembourg.

A more fundamental criticism is that the estimate of the

MPM from equation (1) may be biased due to simultaneity between imports and GNP.[23] As an alternative, equation (1) was re-estimated, using Two-Stage Least Squares (2SLS) and the results are reported in Table 3.2.

TABLE 3.2

	MPM(2SLS)	MPM(b_1)	t
Belgium–Luxembourg	0·577	0·558	0·2773
Denmark	0·264	0·263	0·0229
France	0·155	0·153	0·0604
Germany	0·156	0·160	0·0520
Ireland	0·388	0·389	0·0200
Italy	0·197	0·187	0·2000
Netherlands	0·409	0·402	0·1136
United Kingdom	0·262	0·236	0·5678

Clearly, the results from the two alternative estimation methods are virtually identical, and as the two estimates are insignificantly different for all countries, it can be concluded that any simultaneous equation bias that does exist is not important and has little effect on the results.[24]

Having established a satisfactory measure of openness for all EEC members, it is pertinent to determine whether the individual economies are open enough, in McKinnon's sense, to form a successful currency area. McKinnon, in his concentration on the ratio of tradables to non-tradables, gives no hint of a critical ratio above which an economy can be unambiguously deemed 'open'. This is disappointing and reduces the empirical significance of his contribution, but it is undoubtedly due to his awareness of the blurred distinction in practice between tradable and non-tradable goods: ' ... in practice, there is a continuum of goods between the tradable and non-tradable extremes. The relaxation of this sharp distinction does not invalidate the basic idea of the openness of the economy affecting optimum economic policies; but the empirical measurement of the ratio of tradable to non-tradable goods becomes more difficult.'[25]

So a criterion to determine whether an economy is open or not is not available from McKinnon and must be established independent of his contribution. Corden, defining a 'feasible' currency area as one where there is sufficient money illusion following a devaluation to lead to a fall in real wages to make that devaluation successful, believes that all current EEC members except Ireland and Luxembourg are closed enough to have their own currency.[26] Cross and Laidler[27] find that the determinants of inflation in France and West Germany are purely domestic, suggesting they are closed economies, while for the UK international factors play little role in the determination of inflation, suggesting closedness also, and Belgium, Ireland, Italy and the Netherlands display openness characteristics, due to the low weight given to domestic factors in price level determination. Clearly, this study did not set out to make any conclusions on the openness of the economies concerned, but the results are nevertheless very relevant to this issue.[28] Evidence to date therefore suggests that, if anything, some of the economies of the EEC – France, West Germany and the UK – are not open enough to join a successful currency area – they would do better by maintaining their individual currencies.

The results in this study can be re-evaluated in the light of this other evidence. From Tables 3.1 and 3.2, it is clear that Belgium–Luxembourg, Denmark, Ireland and the Netherlands are all open economies, with imports amounting to over 25 per cent of GNP. Of the other members, there is more than a suspicion – particularly if the MPM is used as a guide – that the UK is also 'open'. None of the other economies are closed in the sense that the USA is, with imports accounting for less than 5 per cent of GNP, but whether they are open enough to satisfy McKinnon's criterion is less clear. Despite the earlier evidence of Corden and Cross and Laidler, it may be valid to say that all the EEC economies are sufficiently open to satisfy McKinnon's criterion. That is not to say that some of the members would 'do better' in some sense by joining a currency area, but merely that the establishment of a European Monetary Union would not be a catastrophe for such marginally open economies.

The above conclusion tentatively in favour of EMU on this criterion would be strengthened if there were evidence that the members of the EEC had become more open since joining the Community. This can be sought by comparing the Average Propensity to Import of the EEC members over time. Table 3.3 shows the APMs of the original six member countries for 1958 (the inception of the EEC), 1966, 1972 and 1973, and the APMs of the three new members for 1972 and 1973:

TABLE 3.3

APM of the EEC members (1958–1972, 1973)

	1958	1966	1972	1973
Belgium–Luxembourg	0·2982	0·3928	0·4344	0·5366
Denmark			0·2447	0·2779
France	0·1003	0·1105	0·1349	0·1435
Germany	0·1337	0·1472	0·1550	0·1544
Ireland			0·3892	0·3541
Italy	0·1060	0·1343	0·1634	0·1787
Netherlands	0·3808	0·3842	0·3838	0·4022
UK			0·1842	0·2330
Weighted Average $\text{APM} = \dfrac{\dfrac{Mt}{Yt}}{n}$	0·1422	0·1611	0·1814	0·2012
SD	0·1039	0·1127	0·1145	0·1288

Between 1958 and 1973 all the original six members increased their APMs – partly, presumably, as a result of the removal of many barriers of trade – with the rise in the figure for Belgium–Luxembourg being particularly remarkable. In addition, only Ireland of the three new members did not experience a sizeable increase in her dependence on trade between 1972 and 1973 – after only one year of membership. This increased dependence on trade should become more noticeable after a number of years' membership of the Community. Table 3.3 also shows the 'average' APM for each year obtained by summing imports and GNP over each country. (This, of course, is not interpretable as an EEC APM, as a large part of the data will represent intra-trade and so will be double-counted.) This figure with the individual country evidence confirms that the openness of the EEC economies is increasing, and while doubt does still remain as to whether openness of these economies is sufficient, the dependence on trade of each EEC member is gradually increasing. McKinnon's criterion may not be unambiguously satisfied yet, but it surely will be when the time comes to establish EMU. In addition, the standard deviations of the APMs are reported for each year. These show that the experience of the EEC economies in relation to openness is not converging over time. Some evidence of convergence would have been a considerable argument in favour of EMU, but this result is not really unexpected. This is because there is not a great deal of change in the APMs of the relatively closed economies, e.g. France and Germany, to counterbalance the tremendous increase in the APMs of the smaller countries such as Belgium–Luxembourg and the Netherlands. It is only to be expected that the dispersion of these figures has increased between 1958 and 1973.

It can also be implied from McKinnon's theory that, in addition to openness, a large degree of trade dependence or interpenetration between the member countries of a currency area would be helpful. This is because high trade dependence between countries should help adjustment to balance of payments disequilibria without recourse to exchange rate variations, except in the case of structural demand shifts within the currency area itself. This is a totally separate issue from that of openness – a fact perhaps not always appreciated[29] – and fortunately evidence on it is both easier to obtain and more conclusive. Tables 3.4 and 3.5 show the percentage of exports and imports going to another member of the Community in that country's total exports and imports, for various years from 1958 to 1973. (The figures in brackets refer to the percentage of exports or imports going to the EEC as it has been since 1973, while the appropriate figure for 1973 refers to the nine members only.) This evidence shows conclusively that intra-EEC trade is both very important and growing. Only the UK does appreciably less than 50 per cent of its trade with other members of the EEC (and this figure is increasing), while countries such as Belgium, Ireland (mainly with the UK) and the Netherlands carry on as much as two-thirds of their trade with other members of the EEC. These are remark-

TABLE 3.4

Percentage of trade with other members of the EEC Six (Nine): exports

	1958	1966	1972	1973
Belgium–Luxembourg	45·12 (52·81)	62·88 (68·99)	68·43 (73·92)	72·95
France	22·17 (27·96)	42·29 (47·97)	49·26 (55·74)	54·78
Germany	27·33 (34·49)	36·36 (43·41)	39·90 (46·95)	47·10
Italy	23·61 (31·27)	40·65 (46·17)	45·13 (50·28)	50·69
Netherlands	41·55 (56·53)	55·55 (65·89)	64·42 (73·68)	72·41
Denmark	32·66 (58·28)	24·48 (47·83)	26·55 (49·98)	54·16
Ireland	4·64 (81·57)	11·01 (80·90)	15·60 (77·00)	75·00
UK	13·79 (19·62)	19·92 (26·14)	23·06 (30·37)	32·59

TABLE 3.5

Percentage of trade with other members of the EEC Six (Nine): imports

	1958	1966	1972	1973
Belgium–Luxembourg	46·62 (55·43)	55·88 (64·02)	64·43 (71·46)	71·95
France	21·87 (26·11)	40·87 (46·57)	50·00 (55·91)	54·88
Germany	25·59 (33·40)	38·23 (44·62)	48·63 (53·71)	51·92
Italy	21·38 (29·05)	32·56 (38·24)	44·88 (49·20)	49·17
Netherlands	41·87 (49·97)	54·03 (60·98)	56·50 (62·52)	60·53
Denmark	36·19 (58·71)	35·30 (52·04)	33·37 (45·74)	46·24
Ireland	11·10 (68·11)	13·49 (66·22)	17·35 (69·16)	78·67
UK	14·17 (20·11)	18·53 (25·12)	24·38 (31·46)	32·71

TABLE 3.6

Annual growth rate of member countries' exports and imports
to other EEC members and the world, 1958–73

| | Exports | | Imports | |
	EEC	World	EEC	World
Belgium–Luxembourg	15·97	12·82	15·44	12·59
Denmark	9·24	9·78	10·90	11·44
France	17·90	13·05	18·03	11·93
Germany	16·04	13·77	18·26	13·20
Ireland	17·56	10·96	15·25	10·95
Italy	18·02	13·56	17·96	12·90
Netherlands	16·61	13·58	13·76	11·75
UK	10·98	7·60	13·27	8·49

able testaments to the appropriateness of the EEC, given the large amounts of raw materials – in particular oil – that at present must be imported by all these countries from outside Europe. The growth in trade interpenetration can be confirmed by observing the annual growth rates of trade with the EEC and with the world of all EEC members. Table 3.6 shows these rates of growth for imports and exports from 1958 to 1973.

The picture conveyed in Tables 3.4 and 3.5 of an increasing percentage of each member's trade being with the EEC is confirmed by these growth rates. Only Denmark – which was not a member of the EEC over the majority of the data period, of course – shows a greater growth in trade in total than of trade with other EEC countries. These very slightly exaggerate the role of the relaxation of trade restrictions in these figures. This is because with increasing transport costs, it is to be expected that an increasing proportion of a country's trade will be conducted with geographically local countries. However, the differential rates of growth in Table 3.6 are unlikely to be explained completely by this factor.

Interpenetration in trade is clearly very high and increasing, and if McKinnon is to be believed, this is a considerable aid to intra-EEC adjustment of disequilibria. On this basis, too, there are no other obvious candidates for EEC membership. The USA is the only country outside the present

Community which has important – in quantitative terms – trading links with most EEC countries. Trade interpenetration would not therefore increase by much if the proposed currency area were to embrace other European countries as well as the EEC. This criterion is, empirically, considerably more hopeful for the EEC than is that of factor mobility. There is much evidence of increasingly important trade links, such that the establishment of EMU would create a currency area which approached optimality in the sense used in these theories.

DIVERSIFICATION
The contribution of Kenen[30] to the optimal currency area debate concentrated on the diversification of a country's output. His major argument was that a country with a highly diversified industrial base could forego exchange rate changes, as such a country is unlikely to suffer a recession due to a shift in demand away from one product or group of products. This theory, although plausible on theoretical grounds, has been criticised for its extreme assumptions.[31] It is also something less than operational for two reasons. First, how is 'diversity in a nation's product mix' to be measured? Kenen's approach is to calculate the number of single-product regions in a single country. This idea draws on the earlier contribution of Mundell[32] by concentrating on the delineation of a country into regions between which factors are immobile, and within which factors are mobile. Clearly this is an appropriate measure in theory but is not very helpful in the evaluation of a group of countries from this angle. How does one identify a single-product region in practice? Secondly, as with the theory of McKinnon, what is the critical value above which a country satisfies this particular criterion of diversity, such that that country can forego the ability to change its exchange rate? These are very vital empirical issues which make the evaluation of the EEC as a proposed currency area in the light of Kenen's theory a hazardous undertaking.

Such opinion as has been expressed to date is divided. Reitsma[33] states categorically that 'the EEC countries have diversified economies', without saying if that diversification is sufficient to satisfy Kenen's criterion. Balassa[34] outlines a major difference between regions in the USA, where individual industries are often concentrated, and France, Germany, Italy and the UK, each of which has 'a full complement of industries'. Clearly, McKinnon's and Kenen's theories are going to conflict empirically as well as theoretically, as this evidence implies that the closed economies are well-diversified, while the open ones are not. Wood[35] outlines the major problem – 'we can not say how much diversity is enough'. Kenen's only advice on this point is vague, although he does state that the principal well developed economies in the world are sufficiently well diversified for the satisfaction of his criterion. But, which countries in the EEC are covered by this statement?

This clearly is an unsatisfactory state of affairs. The only information on the diversification of EEC members' outputs is based on hunch and speculation, with little, if any, empirical backing. These exercises suggest that France, Germany, Italy and the UK and (perhaps?) Belgium and the Netherlands are sufficiently well diversified to lose, without cost, the ability to alter exchange rates. Almost any empirical evidence should relieve this uncertainty somewhat. Data can be obtained[36] on the industrial origin of the GDP in all EEC countries. The percentage contribution of each of eleven sectors to the GDP was calculated. A diversification statistic (DS) was computed as the number of sectors which contributed more than one-eleventh or 9·09 per cent to GDP. Clearly, a perfectly diversified economy would have a DS of 11 and an economy concentrated in only one sector a DS of 1. The greater is the diversification of a country's GDP, the larger should be this statistic.[37] Table 3.7 shows the value of this statistic for each EEC member for 1971:

TABLE 3.7

Diversification Statistic

Belgium	4	Italy	4
Denmark	5	Luxembourg	3
France	5	Netherlands	4
Germany	3	UK	5
Ireland	3		

As a check on this procedure, the standard deviation of the percentage contributions of each sector in the GDP was calculated for each country. The correlation coefficient between the DS and the standard deviation should be negative for the higher is the DS the lower the variability in each sector's contribution. The value of this coefficient for 1971 was -0.696, which is a satisfactory result. This experiment suggests, firstly, that the experience of the EEC members on diversification is less variable than might be expected. Secondly, it seems that Denmark, France and the UK are the most diversified economies in the EEC, with Germany, Ireland and Luxembourg the least diversified. These results – apart from those for Denmark and Germany – are believable. One would expect that Denmark is not well diversified, while Germany is so.

This strange result for these two countries does cast a doubt on the procedure. A second problem is whether the eleven sectors outlined reflect output diversification in a way appropriate to Kenen's model. The fact that all manufacturing is included in one sector may be a particular problem. A breakdown of this sector into manufacturing groupings would have probably achieved a better result, but this was not possible with the data available. This procedure is certainly of some value in the analysis of Kenen's approach – but does it tell us whether the criterion is actually satisfied in all or only some of the EEC countries? Intuitively and with the help of the empirical work, doubts must surely be expressed about the suitability of Luxembourg (although not Belgium – Luxembourg) and Ireland as members of an EEC currency area on the basis of this approach.

However, it is true that in a monetary union in the EEC, the Community as a whole would be highly diversified and would satisfy Kenen's criterion even if some individual members do not.

INFLATION AND UNEMPLOYMENT

The theories of Mundell, McKinnon and Kenen clearly present some problems on the feasibility and optimality of the EEC as a currency area, as well as contributing some tentative conclusions on the issue. Looked at as a whole, these theories lose some relevance because of their concentration on automatic or semi-automatic forces to attain equilibrium and hence optimality. The intervention of government can make only marginal impact on the degree of factor mobility, openness and diversity of product-mix in any economy. Emphasis in the remainder of this chapter will therefore be placed on the approaches to the currency area issue which concentrate on adjustment through government policy. In particular, these approaches have concentrated on the position, slope and stability of the trade-off between the traditional policy targets of low inflation and low unemployment.

EMU, envisaged as involving completely fixed exchange rates, could leave some countries suffering from balance of payments disequilibria and unable to alter exchange rates to rectify this. A common currency would mean the manifestation of these disequilibria as regional imbalances so that a currency area must use the ability to obtain internal and external balance without exchange rate adjustment as a prerequisite of monetary union. If automatic adjustments, via factor mobility to remove imbalance, or openness or diversity to minimise the domestic impact of imbalance, cannot be relied on, government policy must be used to minimise this problem of disequilibria. In a fixed exchange rate or common currency world, balance of payments disequilibria can only be avoided by the adoption by each country of a common inflation rate. In fact, traditionally, in the long run, all countries in a fixed exchange rate world exhibit a common inflation rate.[38]

Evidence on the historical record of individual EEC member inflation rates cannot, of course, be taken as a firm guide to future movements. However, the figures in Table 3.8 show that the discrepancies between member inflation rates from 1959 to 1974 were considerable. Even computing five-year moving averages of recent inflation rates does not remove the divergent behaviour,[39] while, more seriously, the projections for 1970–5,[40] although showing some convergence, have not been borne out in practice with inflation rates both galloping ahead and becoming more disparate between members. The condition of equal inflation rates has

TABLE 3.8
EEC inflation rates, 1959–74

Year	Belg–Lux	Denmark	France	West Germany	Ireland	Italy	Neths	UK	X^2 value
1959	1·18	1·82	5·74	1·00	0·00	−0·47	0·89	0·56	15·8130
1960	0·31	1·20	4·12	1·21	0·43	2·35	2·54	1·01	6·9540
1961	0·94	3·54	2·38	2·49	2·75	2·06	1·61	3·41	2·2097
1962	1·45	7·28	5·21	2·98	4·26	4·62	1·90	4·26	6·1786
1963	2·14	6·16	5·15	2·88	2·47	7·53	3·84	1·93	7·4299
1964	4·20	3·11	3·10	2·40	6·70	5·90	5·50	3·30	4·0306
1965	4·04	5·43	2·72	3·13	4·97	3·58	3·99	4·74	1·4843
1966	4·14	7·08	2·64	3·78	3·03	3·32	7·02	3·98	4·7536
1967	2·93	8·08	2·76	1·64	3·12	3·62	3·40	2·49	7·5567
1968	2·78	8·04	4·56	2·25	4·80	1·37	3·83	4·68	7·2343
1969	3·66	3·64	6·07	1·90	7·44	2·69	7·34	5·38	6·4772
1970	3·95	6·50	5·93	3·41	8·23	4·93	3·63	6·38	3·6949
1971	4·30	5·80	5·50	5·30	8·90	4·80	7·50	9·40	4·0045
1972	5·47	6·62	5·88	5·51	8·63	5·73	7·81	7·13	1·4631
1973	7·00	9·31	7·34	6·93	11·50	10·83	8·02	9·13	2·4220
1974	12·66	15·33	13·39	6·99	16·91	19·06	9·66	16·03	7·9697

Source: *International Financial Statistics*, Washington supplement to 1972 ed. (March 1975).

clearly not been satisfied to date.

The explanation of these widely divergent inflationary experiences is crucial but, unfortunately, is also subject to considerable controversy. The traditional Keynesian account is that structural factors are the major determinants of a country's inflation rate, such that each country has a different national 'propensity to inflate' (NPI).[41] In this approach, the government's ability to control the inflation rate is limited to any influence it has on inflation expectations, assuming that 'structural' factors are independent of policy. If this view is correct, there is little likelihood that the divergent performances of the EEC countries on inflation will be brought together, unless these structural influences on inflation are similar in the EEC or are likely to converge. Such convergence may be possible through such developments as Community-wide collective bargaining procedures, a Community regional policy and, in general, an attempt to 'Europeanise' industrial and social institutions of various types. Rather than having to hold out hope for these very intangible developments, it is more encouraging that such a structural explanation of inflation awaits empirical validation. The classic work on the effect of trade union militancy on wage inflation in the UK[42] has recently been heavily attacked,[43] while Ward and Zis found little role for militancy in a number of advanced countries, including all members of the EEC, except Denmark, Ireland and Luxembourg.[44]

A second explanation of divergent inflation experiences in the EEC relies on the different degrees of expansion in government policy. In particular, the monetarist school believes that changes in the money stock (assumed to be under government control) will lead after a time-lag to changes in, first output, and then prices. The divergent price level movements in the EEC could therefore be removed, after a time-lag, by introducing a common rate of growth of the money supply.[45] Such a view is backed up by empirical evidence by Parkin[46] of a familiar type in these days of 'monetarist counter-revolution', something which is notably lacking from the structural or institutional explanation of inflation. Any country that allowed its money stock to grow faster (slower) than the target rate would be confronted with a balance of payments deficit (surplus). In the absence of the exchange rate as an adjustment weapon, that country must seek equilibrium by cutting back (increasing) its monetary growth to the target level. Wood argues[47] that devaluation by cutting export prices is a more successful weapon for a country in deficit than is monetary contraction because domestic prices are sticky downwards. Adjustment to a cut in the money supply comes, hence, from increased unemployment – a quantity adjustment – with, perhaps, a reduction in prices in the long run. The argument against the monetarist view is often not over its validity, which empirical evidence has established very strongly, but over its consequences in terms of increased unemployment for a deficit country.

Such problems could be avoided if the target inflation rate were adhered to. Even in such a situation, however, different rates of unemployment will be experienced by member countries, due to the existence of different trade-offs between unemployment and inflation. Such trade-offs will, except by coincidence, be different for all member countries.[48] Fleming[49] has highlighted the probability that the slope and position of every country's Phillips' Curve will differ, leading to different levels of unemployment being experienced at the target inflation rate. Intuitively, Onida states that 'labour supply conditions in countries like Germany and Italy are so far apart that any reasonable guess points to quite different rates of growth of potential output and a different inflation–unemployment|trade-off'.[50] More rigorously, the majority of the empirical work on this trade-off has concentrated on its stability and predictive power rather than the slope of the trade-off. The stability of the relationship was undeniable, until the recent rise in the inflation rate, for virtually all countries studied.[51] Recent work for the UK[52] and for ten industrialised countries including all members of the EEC except Denmark, Ireland and Luxembourg,[53] has evidence for the continued stability of the relation, while Nordhaus[54] and Laidler and Corry[55] find no recent evidence for the naïve Phillips' Curve relationship between unemployment and wage inflation.

To investigate this relationship, the following equation

was fitted for all EEC members:

$$W_i = \alpha \mid \beta U_i + \epsilon^{56} \tag{5}$$

the aim being to compare the values of α and β in order to gauge the discrepancies between members as to the position and slope of the trade-offs involved. The results are reported in Table 3.9, with t-statistics shown in parentheses.

TABLE 3.9

	α	β	$\bar{R}^2$	D–W
Belgium–Luxembourg	15·40	−2·070	0·2964	0·3197
		(2·71)		
Denmark	15·23	−1·079	0·2611	1·2297
		(2·51)		
France	4·16	3·016	0·2534	1·3791
		(2·47)		
Germany	10·13	−1·927	0·2450	1·0047
		(2·42)		
Ireland	4·65	0·775	−0·0502	1·1227
		(0·53)		
Italy	21·80	−3·298	0·2121	1·1180
		(2·24)		
Netherlands	8·67	0·363	−0·0652	1·0604
		(0·29)		
UK	−1·55	3·451	0·4488	1·4990
		(3·64)		

Note: D–W = Durbin–Watson statistic.

These results cast doubt on the empirical validity of the Phillips' curve over this period. The widely differing trade-off situations can be observed (on Figure 3.1) such that if an inflation rate of 5 per cent were agreed upon, the resultant unemployment levels would be:[57]

Belgium–Luxembourg	5·024
Denmark	9·481
France	0·279
Germany	2·662
Ireland	0·452
Italy	5·094
Netherlands	−10·110
UK	1·898

The inverse relationship between inflation and unemployment is a myth for France, Ireland, the Netherlands and
the United Kingdom. Clearly, from this test of the naïve
short-run Phillips' relationship, the ability to choose a common inflation rate is of little value for the EEC, because of
the wide diversity of trade-offs.

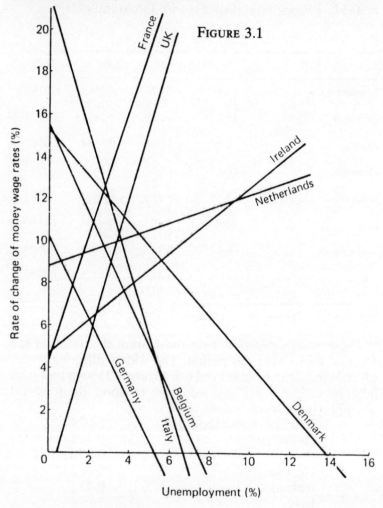

FIGURE 3.1

Another very important issue is the choice of the inflation rate itself. Even if by strict monetarist methods and suitable convergence of 'structural' factors, a common trade-off resulted, the choice of the 'optimal' position on the trade-off may be a source of dispute. This is particularly relevant as it is well known that Germany – remembering the 1920s – prefers a lower inflation rate than the United Kingdom – remembering the 1930s.[58] It is likely therefore that the disparate inflation records of the last fifteen years reported in Table 3.8 are as much the result of differing preferences between unemployment and inflation as of different inherent trade-offs amongst the member countries. The EEC members do not have a good history of agreement on economic matters as exemplified by the often nationalistic reactions to the international monetary situations of the 1970s, and 'the political problem of getting countries to agree on an inflation rate for the whole of Europe'[59] may be more intractable than Parkin seems to believe. This extra problem is the conclusive one, in fact, for Onida,

> . . . if in addition we allow for different views of single member countries' governments as to their preferences between unemployment and inflation (as against the transformation function, shown by the Phillips' Curve) the probability of divergent trade performances becomes *decisively* high.[60]

THE LONG-RUN PHILLIPS' CURVE

Sumner [61] has defined an optimal currency area, in the light of this trade-off debate, as the largest area within which the optimal inflation rate is uniform. Under this criterion the EEC has not qualified to date as an optimal currency area. Fortunately, through the pioneering work of Phelps and Friedman there is increasing doubt over the long-run slope of the Phillips' relationship.[62] The trade-off still exists in the short run but will either become much steeper or completely vertical in the long run, due in the latter case to the absence of money illusion and a situation of perfectly anticipated inflation. If inflation is only imperfectly anticipated, such that some money illusion does still exist, the arguments of the last section still apply and the case for EMU remains unproven. The essence of this hypothesis of the long-run Phillips' Curve, is that *any* level of inflation is compatible with the *natural* level of unemployment. If an attempt is made to run the economy below this 'natural' level of unemployment inflation will accelerate, and if the economy is run at an unemployment level above the 'natural' one inflation will decelerate. Clearly, the vital empirical issues for the EEC are:

(a) Does a trade-off between inflation and unemployment exist in the long run for each member?
(b) If not, what is the natural level of unemployment in the individual member countries?

It is to these issues that the debate now turns.

The work of Phelps and Friedman leads to the hypothesis that workers – who can only bargain in money wage terms, but who are aware of their real wage situation – will seek to adjust wages in accordance with excess demand and the expected rate of price change.

$$\dot{w} = f(ED, \dot{p}^e) \qquad (6)$$

Where ED is excess demand and $\dot{p}^e$ the expected rate of change of prices. It is predicted that the coefficient on $\dot{p}^e$ in a regression of equation (6) will be unity, showing that inflation is perfectly anticipated. In Phillips' Curve terms, where excess demand is proxied by unemployment, the short-run trade-off will be negative (1 in Figure 3.2) still, but will shift upwards and to the right as price expectations increase with the long-run relation being vertical (2 in Figure 3.2) above the natural level of unemployment (UN).

If inflation were imperfectly anticipated, a trade-off would exist in the long run also (3 in Figure 3.2) but would be steeper than the short-run trade-off.

WAGE EQUATION TESTS

Numerous tests have been completed on equation (6) and variants of it. The major problem with a simple test of (6) is the inability to observe price expectations. Two approaches have been used to surmount this difficulty. Firstly, attempts have been made to measure price expectations directly, using qualitative data on, for example, businessmen's expec-

FIGURE 3.2

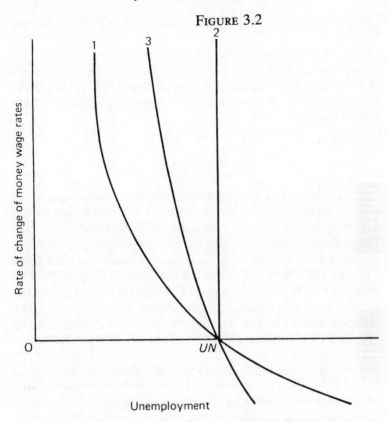

Unemployment

tations of inflation collected by the CBI in the United Kingdom, or individual expectations collected by the Gallup Poll.[63] Of the EEC members, such a procedure in an equation like (6) has only been adopted for the UK. Parkin, Sumner and Ward find that the coefficient on $\dot{p}^e$ is insignificantly different from unity, suggesting that a long-run trade-off does not exist.[64] This approach was not used in this study due to the lack of consistent data on price expectations for each EEC member.

A second test of the no long-run trade-off view is to postulate a hypothesis for the determination of $\dot{p}^e$ such that a simple substitution will produce an equation entirely in observable variables. Unfortunately, such methods, using *ex post* proxies for $\dot{p}^e$, perform less well than models in which price expectations are directly measured – at least for the UK.[65]

Naïve Models
A simple method of removing the unobservable price expectations variable is to proxy it by lagged or current actual price changes.

$$\dot{w}_t = f_1(U, \dot{p}_t)$$

$$\dot{w}_t = f_2(U, \dot{p}_{t-1})$$

Lipsey and Parkin, in a study primarily investigating the role of incomes policy on the rate of wage inflation in the UK,[66] found a coefficient on $\dot{p}_t$ which varied from 0·227 for the policy-on period to 0·482 for the whole period. This conclusion in favour of a long-run trade-off for data from 1945 to 1968 is in opposition to that earlier cited of Parkin, Sumner and Ward (data period 1956(2) to 1971(4)), but the apparent contradiction could be due to the effect of higher inflation since 1968 in moving the long-run Phillips' Curve towards a vertical straight line. Inflation is likely to be better anticipated as actual price changes increase. Evidence for Italy from Modiglinani and Tarantelli[67] shows coefficients on actual price changes of just over unity, with the expectations hypothesis of Phelps and Friedman vindicated.

The hypothesis that expected price changes can be proxied by current actual price changes was tested for all EEC countries, therefore by fitting the following equations:[68]

$$\dot{w}_t = \alpha + \beta U_t + \delta \dot{p}_t^e + \epsilon_t \qquad (7)$$

$$\dot{p}_t^e = \dot{p}_t \qquad (8)$$

$$\dot{w}_t = \alpha + \beta U_t + \delta \dot{p}_t + \epsilon_t \qquad (9)$$

As a test of the expectations hypothesis this has two drawbacks. First, it is a very mechanistic, simplistic and essentially convenient way of removing the unobservable p^e. Secondly, a hypothesis that the expected price change in time period t is exactly equal to the actual price change is suspect, as price expectations are formed *ex-ante*, while actual prices

are, of course, *ex-post*.
The results are set out in Table 3.10.

TABLE 3.10

–	α	β	δ	$\bar{R}^2$	D–W
Belgium/Luxembourg	15·255	−2·012	−0·004	0·2496	0·3374
		(2·49)	(0·36)		
Denmark	8·845	−0·491	0·737	0·4576	1·6574
		(1·12)	(2·46)		
France	0·858	3·299	0·541	0·6849	1·5691
		(4·14)	(4·49)		
Germany	6·737	−1·334	0·868	0·4421	1·2399
		(1·84)	(2·44)		
Ireland	3·048	−0·051	1·403	0·7355	2·6870
		(0·07)	(6·53)		
Italy	3·593	−0·645	2·035	0·7107	1·6232
		(0·62)	(5·01)		
Netherlands	5·764	−1·374	1·263	0·6032	2·2623
		(1·62)	(4·96)		
UK	−0·538	1·029	1·074	0·7958	2·0528
		(1·36)	(4·98)		

The results are satisfactory except for Belgium, where $\dot{p}_t$ has the wrong sign, and for France and the UK, where the short-run Phillips' Curve is again found to be positively sloped. They are a considerable improvement on those results in Table 3.9 and show the importance of price changes in wage determination for all countries except Belgium, where unemployment dominates. More interestingly, a unit coefficient on $\dot{p}_t$ cannot be rejected for Denmark, Germany, Ireland, the Netherlands and the UK, while for Italy there is the unusual result that price changes seem to be 'over-allowed for' in wage negotiations such that the long-run Phillips' Curve is positively sloped! The Belgian equation can be discounted as it appears from the low significance level of δ and the continued presence of auto-correlation in the residuals, that this proxy for $\dot{p}^e$ is inadequate. Only, therefore, for France and the special case of Italy is there evidence that the long-run Phillips' Curve is not vertical.

The alternative mechanistic assumption that expected

price changes are proxied by lagged actual price changes ($\dot{p}_{t-1}$) is intuitively more satisfactory as movements of the price level in $t-1$ can then be used to form (at the beginning of period t) expectations about prices in t. This scheme was used by Duck *et al.*[69] as one of a number of alternative expectational hypotheses for their study of the determination of the 'world' inflation rate. A coefficient of 0·86 was obtained on the price variable such that a vertical long-run relationship could not be rejected, and the whole equation was not markedly inferior to those containing more complex specifications of $\dot{p}^e$. In a study by the OECD of six countries[70] (including France, Germany and the UK), Germany alone of the three EEC members had a unit coefficient on $\dot{p}_{t-1}$, although for Germany and the UK a GNP deflator was used and not the retail price index. Both Brechling[71] and Nordhaus[72] used a series of lagged prices on the assumption that expectations are formed from a number of previous periods, not merely the most recent one, i.e.

$$p_t^i = \tau \sum_{i=1}^{T} (\dot{p}_{t-1})^{\lambda i} \qquad (10)$$

such that $\tau \sum_{i=1}^{T} \lambda i = 1$.

Nordaus assumed that the inflation rate in $t-7$ had some influence on $\dot{p}_t^e$ and so truncated after seven years.

In Brechling's work the sum of the coefficients on the price variables is insignificantly different from unity for the UK. This result is at odds with that of the OECD, and no clear picture emerges from this series of work.

The following hypothesis was therefore tested for all EEC countries:

$$\dot{w}_t = \alpha + \beta U_t + \delta \dot{p}_t^e + \epsilon_t \qquad (7)$$

$$\dot{p}_t^e = \dot{p}_{t-1} \qquad (11)$$

$$\dot{w}_t = \alpha + \beta U_t + \delta \dot{p}_{t-1} + \epsilon_t \qquad (12)$$

The results are set out in Table 3.11.

TABLE 3.11

–	α	β	δ	$\bar{R}^2$	D–W
Belgium–Luxembourg	15·443	−2·063	−0·004	0·2494	0·3808
		(2·61)	(0·35)		
Denmark	12·745	−0·957	0·406	0·2967	1·4466
		(2·23)	(1·31)		
France	4·892	3·183	−0·209	0·2831	0·9598
		(2·64)	(1·26)		
Germany	8·885	−1·877	0·429	0·2299	1·1105
		(2·33)	(0·85)		
Ireland	8·755	−0·626	1·148	0·2253	2·3628
		(0·45)	(2·45)		
Italy	15·265	−2·435	0·951	0·2283	1·3218
		(1·49)	(1·14)		
Netherlands	7·707	−0·572	0·556	−0·0336	1·4058
		(0·39)	(1·20)		
UK	0·146	1·248	0·868	0·5110	1·8236
		(0·78)	(1·67)		

The results are much inferior to those in Table 3.10, suggesting that contemporaneous actual price changes are a more valid proxy for $\dot{p}^e_t$ than are lagged prices, despite their interpretative problem. The fit is worse due to the smaller role of lagged prices in current wage determination, and the equations for Belgium, France and the UK are again unsatisfactory. However, on the positive side, the results confirm the vindication of the expectations hypothesis for Germany, Ireland, the Netherlands and the UK, while the same applies to Denmark but only at the 90 per cent confidence level. The price coefficient for Italy is also more acceptable, and there is no evidence of a long-run trade-off for that country either.

These simple convenient tests of the expectations-augmented Phillips' relation have been encouraging. The hypothesis on expectations formation was invalid for Belgium and France, but for all other countries there is evidence that in the long run the Phillips' Curve – whatever its short-run slope – is vertical.

Adaptive Expectations
A more plausible – but also more complex – method of testing the expectations hypothesis without measuring $\dot{p}^e$ is

to make use of the familiar error-learning mechanism, where expectations are assumed to be formed by correcting the most recent 'error' represented by the divergence between previous actual and expected inflation. A typical hypothesis of this type is:

$$\dot{p}_t^e = \dot{p}_{t-1}^e + \lambda(\dot{p}_{t-1} - \dot{p}_{t-1}^e) \tag{13}$$

$$= \lambda\dot{p}_{t-1} + (1-\lambda)\dot{p}_{t-1}^e \tag{14}$$

$$0 \leqslant \lambda \leqslant 1$$

where λ is the adjustment parameter. Substituting in (7) for $\dot{p}_t^e$ and utilising a Koyck transformation[73] leads to the estimating equation (15):

$$\dot{w}_t = a_0 + a_1 U_t + a_2 U_{t-1} + a_3 \dot{p}_{t-1} + a_4 \dot{w}_{t-1} + \epsilon_t \tag{15}$$

with
$$a_0 = \alpha\lambda$$
$$a_1 = \beta$$
$$a_2 = -\beta(1-\lambda)$$
$$a_3 = \delta\lambda$$
$$a_4 = 1-\lambda$$

The justification for this approach comes in part from the obvious relevance of an expectations-formation scheme utilising previous information, and partly from some empirical vindication of it. Carlson and Parkin[74] estimated (14) for observed data on expectations from 1960 to 1971 and found that the restriction that the coefficients on $\dot{p}_{t-1}$ and $\dot{p}_{t-1}^e$ sum to unity was not rejected:

$$\dot{p}_t^e = 0 \cdot 134\dot{p}_{t-1} + 0 \cdot 862\dot{p}_{t-1}^e \qquad \bar{R}^2 = 0 \cdot 70$$
$$(2 \cdot 43) \qquad (16 \cdot 826) \quad \text{D–W} = 2 \cdot 271$$

A higher order scheme suggested by Rose[75] has also been found to be important, taking into account the two previous errors:

$$\dot{p}_t^e = \dot{p}_{t-1}^e + \lambda_1(\dot{p}_{t-1} - \dot{p}_{t-1}^e) + \lambda_2(\dot{p}_{t-2} - \dot{p}_{t-2}^e) \tag{16}$$

This approach has, however, been heavily criticised as a method of forming expectations, for a number of reasons. First, the adaptive expectations hypothesis postulates that expected prices are proxied by an exponentially weighted average of past rates of inflation with the weights declining through time. It may not be valid to assume that events in $t-1$ have a greater effect on p^e than those in $t-2$. Secondly, the assumption that the weights sum to unity has been criticised by Sargent.[76] If the weights sum to 1 and inflation is accelerating, then price expectations will always lag behind the actual rate of inflation such that the estimate of p^e formed in this way under-values the true figure.[77] A unit sum assumption is valid if inflation starts at 0 per cent, moves up to 1 and then remains constant. A third problem is that the adjustment parameter (λ_i) must be equal for all members of the population to validate this hypothesis.[78] Clearly, this is an assumption which is unlikely to hold. Different people will adjust in different ways for a previous error in p^e. Finally, and most seriously, it has been convincingly demonstrated by Saunders and Nobay[79] that the same reduced form estimating equation can be obtained from an alternative expectations scheme.

Despite these theoretical problems with the error-learning approach to the price expectations formation, Carlson and Parkin[80] find that for the UK such a process, where the last two errors are important, outperforms any other hypothesis tested, including a string of 'other' variables, such as changes in the political party in power, incomes policy and indirect taxation changes. The only other variable to affect price expectations significantly is the exchange rate. Such a result is a surprisingly strong vindication of error-learning mechanisms and of the work done using them to test the expectations hypothesis. Parkin, using a simple first-order adaptive expectations scheme, found a coefficient on $\dot{p}^e$ varying from 0·44 to 0·65,[81] but his conclusion in favour of a long-run trade-off for the UK was the basis of the criticism of Saunders and Nobay noted earlier. These authors in fact hypothesised an alternative expectations structure and reworked the Parkin model to obtain a conclusion against a long-run trade-off. They conclude that use of an adaptive expectations scheme could therefore bias downwards the coefficient on $\dot{p}^e$. Duck *et al.*[82] find evidence in favour of a vertical Phillips' curve for the world economy, while most encouragingly for EMU, Cross and Laidler[83] find that for each EEC member the coefficient on $\dot{p}^e$ is insignificantly different from unity.[84]

The problem with estimating equation (15) is that it is over-identified with five coefficients and only four structural parameters. The constraint

$$a_1 a_4 = -a_2 \qquad (15a)$$

must hold. Due to the use of annual data, a constrained least squares estimation procedure would be inappropriate. As an alternative, equation (15) was estimated freely to see if the constraint (15a) holds.[85]

The values of $a_1.a_4$ and a_2 are set out below:

	$a_1.a_4$	$-a_2$
Belgium–Luxembourg	−2·8613	−2·2297
Denmark	−0·1921	+0·0076
France	+0·8175	−1·1108
Germany	−1·1838	−0·5663
Ireland	+0·1292	−1·0579
Italy	−2·6492	−4·1562
Netherlands	−0·2095	−0·7692
UK	−2·5978	−4·0490

It is clear that the constraint (15a) is not satisfied for any country in the estimation of equation (15). In fact, the minimum error recorded is for Belgium of 22·07 per cent, which is far too great for the hypothesis to be taken seriously. In addition, four of the equations had one or more incorrect signs – Denmark, France, Germany and Ireland – and only for the UK were all variables both significant and correctly signed. The relevance of this result is minimal due to the non-satisfaction of (15a) for even this well behaved equation.

Using annual data, therefore, for all EEC member countries, one must reject the error-learning mechanism for generating price-expectations depicted in the wage equation. This is an unusual result alongside the vindication of such a scheme in most recent studies, but the conclusiveness of the results do not warrant investigation of different error-learning mechanisms.

Extrapolative Expectations

A final test of the expectations hypothesis in the wage equation employed the assumption that expectations are extrapolative. This asserts that price expectations equal the most recent inflation rate with a correction for the most recent change in the rate:

$$\dot{p}_t^e = \dot{p}_t + f\,(\dot{p}_t - p_{t-1}) \tag{17}$$

The correction or adjustment parameter f will be positive when the forecaster extrapolates the increase in inflation and negative when expectations are regressive such that the rise in the inflation rate is expected to reverse itself. Substituting (17) into (7) gives the estimating equation (18).

$$a_0 + a_1 U_t + a_2 \dot{p}_t + a_3(\dot{p}_t - \dot{p}_{t-1}) + \epsilon_t \tag{18}$$

where $\qquad\qquad a_3 = \delta f$

This has the clear advantage over the adaptive expectations schemes that all variables are observable in (17), and (18) is exactly identified. However, empirically, it appears to be of more doubtful validity. Carlson and Parkin[86] find that a generalised extrapolative scheme was considerably inferior to the error-learning models. The only test to use this scheme is for Canada[87] – and so of doubtful relevance for the EEC – but the results are as good as those obtained from the adaptive expectations scheme and so constitute a justification for the estimation of equation (18). Equation (18) was therefore fitted for each EEC member, and the results are set out in Table 3.12.

Comparing these results with those in Table 3.10 shows that the correction for the previous change in the inflation rate adds something to the model only for France, Germany and Ireland. Only for Germany is a_3 significant, and for all other countries equation (17) reduces to equation (8).[88] The conclusions on the long-run trade-off in Table 3.10 are reproduced as expected, but it is clear that this hypothesis is rejected as the method by which expectations are formed for all countries, except Germany and perhaps France and Ireland.

TABLE 3.12

	$a_0(\alpha)$	$a_1(\beta)$	$a_2(\delta)$	$a_3(\delta f)$	f	$\bar{R}^2$	D–W
Belgium–Luxembourg	15·246	−1·977 (2·37)	−0·012 (0·58)	0·006 (0·47)	−0·5	0·2016	0·4055
Denmark	8·841	−0·493 (1·06)	0·740 (2·21)	−0·009 (0·02)	−0·012	0·4125	1·6481
France	1·466	3·393 (4·32)	0·384 (2·20)	0·133 (1·22)	0·346	0·6960	1·3781
Germany	7·088	−0·977 (1·36)	0·502 (1·24)	1·071 (1·62)	2·133	0·5039	1·8100
Ireland	1·210	0·328 (0·40)	1·224 (4·48)	0·433 (1·05)	0·354	0·7377	2·5563
Italy	4·060	−0·702 (0·63)	1·956 (3·39)	0·118 (0·20)	0·060	0·6877	1·6714
Netherlands	5·532	−1·636 (1·70)	1·411 (4·02)	−0·193 (0·63)	−0·137	0·5839	2·1222
UK	−0·373	0·845 (0·79)	1·143 (3·22)	−0·099 (0·25)	−0·087	0·7799	2·0351

PRICE EQUATION TESTS

A second set of tests of the 'no long-run trade-off' hypothesis postulates that prices adjust to excess demand and the change in price expectations:

$$\dot{p}_t = \alpha + \beta X_t + \delta \dot{p}_t^e \qquad (19)$$

where X_t is excess demand. In the wage equation of the labour market, unemployment was used as a proxy for excess demand with wages adjusting to the difference between the excess demand and supply of labour, and price expectations. In equation (19), excess demand in the goods market is proxied by the deviations in real Gross Domestic Product (GDP) from the trend of the same variable, i.e.

$$X = Y - Y^T \qquad (20)$$

where Y is actual GDP/P

Y^T is trend GDP/P.[89]

Substituting equation (20) into equation (19):

$$\dot{p}_t = \alpha + \beta(Y - Y^T) + \delta \dot{p}^e \qquad (21)$$

where $\beta > 0$ and the test of the expectations hypothesis is again that $\delta = 1$.

Once again, the problem in equation (21) is the measurement of $\dot{p}^e$ or the use of an adequate proxy for it. Directly measured expectations have only been used for the UK, by Smith,[90] who found that the 'no long-run trade-off' hypothesis could not be rejected, while Knöbl[91] found a coefficient on $\dot{p}^e$ of 0·5 for Germany concluding that a long-run trade-off does exist in that country. This method was again eschewed because of the lack of directly observed expectations data for all EEC countries.

Naïve Model

The first test of equation (21) assumes that price expectations can be simply proxied by lagged prices. Combining equation (11) with equation (21):

$$\dot{p}_t = \alpha + \beta X_t + \delta \dot{p}_{t-1} + \epsilon_t \qquad (22)$$

This form was used by Duck *et al.*[92] and they obtained a coefficient of 0·51 on lagged prices and rejected the 'no long-run trade-off' hypothesis. This was confirmed when the test was repeated constraining δ to unity with considerably different results. As a proxy for p^e, lagged prices were found to be much inferior to error-learning processes. An attempt was made to form a conclusion on this by fitting equation (22) for each EEC country, and the results are outlined in Table 3.13.

These results cast some doubt on the role of excess demand, as defined here, in price determination. Belgium and the Netherlands display the seemingly nonsensical result that prices respond inversely to changes in excess demand. The French equation is also unsatisfactory, having a negative price coefficient. However, the hypothesis is clearly vindicated for Germany and Italy, while β is correctly signed though insignificant for Denmark, Ireland and the UK.[93] A really important feature of the results, nevertheless, is the performance of the price coefficient for all countries except France. The no long-run trade-off hypothesis cannot be rejected for any other country, which is a stronger and more conclusive outcome than any obtained in the wage equation studies. If the few theoretical doubts on the relevance of excess demand as defined in equation (20) and the validity of lagged prices as a proxy for current expectations could be removed, EMU must get a boost from this overwhelming evidence that, in the long run, there is no trade-off between unemployment and inflation.

Adaptive Expectations model

As an alternative to the naïve model, an adaptive expectations mechanism for proxying p^e was tried. Such a mechanism has been used for the UK by Solow,[94] for the world economy by Duck *et al.*,[95] and for a group of twenty countries by Cross and Laidler.[96] In a pathbreaking contribution in this field, Solow found the sum of the coefficients on expectational variables to be between 0·85 and 0·9. With such figures the 'no long-run trade-off' hypothesis could not be rejected. However, the validity of his model as a test of this hypothesis has recently been criticised by Friedman.[97] The use of unit labour cost (ULC) along with the degree of capacity utilisation (CU) as proxies for excess demand means that the strict expectations hypothesis would

TABLE 3.13

	α	β	δ	$\bar{R}^2$	D–W
Belgium–Luxembourg	0·165	−0·0006 (0·07)	1·027 (5·59)	0·6651	1·2058
Denmark	1·885	0·130 (0·45)	0·705 (2·62)	0·2809	1·9969
France	7·168	0·128 (5·12)	−0·398 (2·66)	0·6317	1·1005
Germany	0·446	0·032 (3·03)	0·951 (5·49)	0·7236	2·2510
Ireland	1·069	2·677 (0·36)	0·877 (4·01)	0·4850	1·9569
Italy	1·185	0·001 (2·15)	0·833 (3·15)	0·4049	2·1132
Netherlands	2·174	−0·192 (0·68)	0·518 (1·84)	0·0845	1·8478
UK	0·844	0·466 (0·39)	0·877 (3·78)	0·4771	2·1473

have a coefficient on the price variable of less than 1. The inclusion of wages and price expectations as independent variables implies that the model measures only the effect on the margin between prices and wages. Duck *et al.*[98] found that the coefficients on the price variables in the formulations tested were 0·814 and 0·869, which are insignificantly different from zero. Also this hypothesis outperforms the naïve model used by the authors, while placing a unit constraint on the price expectations variable had little effect on the results in this adaptive expectations framework. A more restrictive model was tested by Cross and Laidler.[99] Instead of estimating the coefficient on expected prices, they assumed it to be unity and in fact found that for all countries, except Israel, the assumption is justified by the data. In particular, the expectations hypothesis was borne out for all EEC members, which is a powerful result despite the variable performance in their study, of the excess demand proxy.

The similarity of the Cross and Laidler results with those obtained in the previous section merits an attempt to confirm them in a similar model:

$$\dot{p}_t = \alpha + \beta X_t + \dot{p}^e_{t-1} \qquad (23)$$

$$\dot{p}^e_t = \lambda \dot{p}_t + (1-\lambda)\dot{p}^e_{t-1} \qquad (14a)$$

Contemporaneous excess demand is used in equation (23), as it was felt that using lagged excess demand would introduce a slower adjustment of price determination than deemed desirable using annual data.

Combining equations (23) and (14a):

$$\dot{p}_t = a_0 + a_1 X_t + a_2 X_{t-1} + a_3 \dot{p}_{t-1} + \epsilon_t \qquad (24)$$

The conditions in the model are: $\beta > 0$, $\lambda > 0$, $a_1 > 0$, $a_2 < 0$, and $a_3 = 1$, with the last condition of unity for a_3 constituting a test of the expectations hypothesis. Equation (24) was fitted for all EEC countries; the results are set out in Table 3.14.

These results reproduce the no long-run trade-off result for all countries except France, but the performance of the excess demand variable is again poor. Three of the lagged excess demand variables have the wrong sign, while the role of excess demand is only significant for France, Germany

TABLE 3.14

	a_0	Coefficients on X_t	X_{t-1}	P_{t-1}	$\bar{R}^2$	D–W
Belgium–Luxembourg	0·225	0·012 (0·91)	−0·013 (1·35)	1·036 (5·81)	0·6850	1·3620
Denmark	0·560	0·234 (0·89)	0·580 (2·01)	1·024 (3·53)	0·4171	2·1205
France	6·871	0·078 (1·99)	0·047 (1·60)	−0·358 (2·49)	0·6712	1·1095
Germany	0·268	0·039 (2·70)	−0·011 (0·73)	1·014 (5·15)	0·7131	2·4849
Ireland	1·189	4·122 (0·51)	−4·247 (0·49)	0·843 (3·51)	0·4531	2·0001
Italy	1·087	0·018 (2·34)	−0·0008 (1·19)	0·876 (3·33)	0·4231	2·4301
Netherlands	2·654	0·121 (0·30)	−0·293 (1·082)	0·433 (1·49)	0·0963	2·3061
UK	0·267	0·400 (0·36)	1·982 (1·69)	1·029 (4·38)	0·5423	1·8866

and Italy. However, the overall fit of these equations is surprisingly good for all countries except the Netherlands, which is a factor to balance against the mixed performance of excess demand.

Extrapolative Expectations
A final test of the stability of the price equation was made with the use of an extrapolative expectations hypothesis. Despite the poor performance of this hypothesis in the wage equation, completeness demands its use in this context, as does the inability to find a satisfactory price equation model for all countries to date:

$$\dot{p}_t = \alpha + \beta X_t + \delta \dot{p}_t^e \qquad (19)$$

$$\dot{p}_t^e = \dot{p}_{t-1} + f(\dot{p}_{t-1} - \dot{p}_{t-2}) \qquad (25)$$

The maintained hypothesis is that price expectations are formed on the basis of the previous rate of inflation and its rate of change lagged one period. Combining equations (19) and (25):

$$\dot{p}_t = a_0 + a_1 X_t + a_2 \dot{p}_{t-1} + a_3(\dot{p}_{t-1} - \dot{p}_{t-2}) + \epsilon_t \qquad (26)$$

where $a_3 = \delta f$ with f the adjustment parameter again. The results from estimating (26) are set out in Table 3.15.

Clearly, these results suggest that the extrapolations expectations hypothesis as a proxy for $\dot{p}^e$ is no more acceptable than in the wage equation results. Comparing these results with those in Table 3.13, one finds that France and the Netherlands are the only equations to improve in performance. For all other countries a_3 is insignificant, and the fit for Belgium is completely disrupted by the presence of the rate of change of price inflation as an independent variable. Again, the only positive result is a confirmation of the long-run verticality of the Phillips' Curve for all countries except Belgium and France.

The results of this section can be summarised:
  (i) There is no evidence of any similarity in the short-run trade-offs between unemployment and inflation for EEC countries.
  (ii) To counter this, only Belgium and France display con-

TABLE 3.15

	$a_0(\delta)$	$a_1(\beta)$	$a_2(\delta)$	$a_3(\delta f)$	f	$\bar{R}^2$	$D\text{-}W$
Belgium–Luxembourg	23·822	−0·069 (0·10)	−0·487 (1·05)	0·146 (0·51)	−0·300	−0·1156	2·0311
Denmark	2·263	0·141 (0·48)	0·626 (2·06)	0·178 (0·62)	0·284	0·2456	2·1985
France	6·923	0·107 (3·86)	−0·318 (2·32)	0·200 (2·93)	−0·629	0·7258	1·7411
Germany	0·410	0·032 (2·92)	0·960 (5·18)	−0·007 (0·21)	−0·007	0·7016	2·2089
Ireland	1·195	9·798 (0·86)	0·853 (3·69)	−0·048 (0·26)	−0·056	0·4708	1·9306
Italy	0·738	0·001 (2·19)	0·950 (2·90)	−0·136 (0·64)	−0·143	0·3764	1·8840
Netherlands	0·946	−0·182 (0·68)	0·845 (2·52)	−0·407 (1·61)	−0·482	0·1835	2·1151
UK	0·941	0·465 (0·37)	0·859 (3·48)	0·036 (0·32)	0·042	0·4406	2·2693

sistent evidence in favour of a long-run trade-off.

(iii) The performance of unemployment and deviations from capacity output as proxies for excess demand is rather mixed – of the two, unemployment performs better. Both variables are, however, completely dominated – except for France – by prices as a determinant of wage inflation. This latter result is not a serious handicap, however, to the results on the long-run trade-off. Whatever the nature of any short-run trade-off between excess demand and inflation, it is clear from our studies that there is scant evidence in favour of any long-run trade-off in six out of eight cases.[100]

(iv) In the wage equation, the most valid proxy for p^e appears to come from the simple substitution of actual price changes for p^e. For the price equation, an error-learning mechanism does perform better, but the demise of extrapolative expectations is confirmed.

THE NATURAL RATE OF UNEMPLOYMENT

There is considerable evidence therefore that the first question posed earlier in this section on whether a long-run trade-off exists between inflation and unemployment can be answered negatively, in six out of eight cases. The issue of the measurement of the natural level of unemployment must now be resolved.

As defined earlier, this natural rate defines the level of unemployment (UN) at which prices can move upwards or downwards at a chosen rate. If any other level of unemployment occurs, the path of prices will be explosive either in an upwards or downwards direction.

This natural rate of unemployment – at which excess demand is zero – is independent of demand-management policies. It is

The level that would be ground out by the Walrasian system of general equilibrium equations, provided there is embedded in them the actual structural characteristics of the labour and commodity markets, including market imperfections, stochastic variability in demands and supplies, the cost of gathering information about job vacancies and labour availabilities, the cost of mobility and so on.[101]

This natural rate does not, therefore, imply the need for some members of the labour force to be permanently jobless, although it does mean that there will always be some people involuntarily out of work, but only temporarily – the frictionally unemployed. It would not be constant necessarily, although fairly stable in the short run, and the constituents of it would be ever-changing.[102]

A number of attempts have been made to evaluate this natural rate in numerical terms. The procedure is to evaluate the root of the equation

$$F(u) = 0 \tag{27}$$

for from
$$\dot{w}_t = \alpha + \beta U_t + \delta \dot{p}_t^e \tag{7}$$

if inflation is completely anticipated

$$\dot{w}_t - \alpha - \dot{p}_t^e = 0 \tag{28}$$

with an adjustment of wages above the rate of price expectations equal to labour productivity (α). Parkin, Sumner and Ward[103] estimate that for the UK the value of UN for their constrained equation is 1·7 per cent, and Duck *et al.*[104] find a world value UN of 2·9 per cent, which seems to imply unemployment of about 5 per cent for the USA, 2 per cent for the UK, and even less for Germany and France. Tobin[105] confirms this result for the USA, suggesting a natural rate of 5–6 per cent. These studies are hampered, however, by seemingly arbitrary assumptions on the level of labour productivity, which is a vital figure in these calculations. There is no justification for the figure chosen in the two UK studies.

Prior to evaluating UN for all EEC countries, estimates of annual labour productivity were obtained:[106]

Belgium–Luxembourg	4·05
Denmark	3·81
France	5·51
Germany	4·96
Ireland	4·39
Italy	5·88
Netherlands	3·84
UK	2·73

From these figures for productivity, the natural rate of

unemployment was evaluated from the results in Table 3.11 for each member country. The values of *UN* are set out in Table 3.16.

TABLE 3.16
Natural rate of unemployment

Belgium–Luxembourg	5·523
Denmark	9·336
France	0·194
Germany	2·091
Ireland	6·973
Italy	3·854
Netherlands	6·760
UK	2·071

These figures are reasonable estimates, although those for France and the UK, despite being apparently sensible, present different conclusions than those for other countries. The implication for these two members due to the positive coefficient on U is that if $U > UN$ inflation will accelerate and if $U < UN$ inflation will fall at an increasingly fast rate. This is a perverse result, so the values of *UN* for France and the UK must be treated with suspicion. The values of *UN* for the other six countries are not widely divergent – except perhaps for Denmark – and are probably not too high a price in terms of increased unemployment for the institution of EMU.[107] This is, however, a speculative statement and will depend on the attitude of individual governments.

One problem is that *UN* is clearly not equal to full employment.[108] This could mean that included in this figure is some involuntary unemployment. This is only to be expected, though, as frictional unemployment which is included in *UN* is clearly not voluntary. Another more serious problem has recently been unearthed in a lucid paper by Gray and Lipsey.[109] They argue that if

(i) The $\dot{w}/U$ relation is non-linear and concave upwards due to the greater flexibility of wages in an upwards than a downwards direction, and

(ii) U is not constant but varies around a mean value,

then maintenance of unemployment at *UN* will, in fact, lead to accelerating inflation and there is a unique value for unemployment $(UNN > UN)$ at which inflation is stable. This has the very serious implication that EMU may only be successful with equal inflation values at levels of unemployment above those 'natural' levels in Table 3.16. Empirically, however, a linear form between $\dot{w}$ and U was a better fit for most EEC countries than the double log form, so there is some evidence that the trade-offs between $\dot{w}$ and U are not far removed from being linear. This reduces the significance of the conclusions of Gray and Lipsey for the EEC as they prove that the greater the non-linearity of the trade-offs, the greater the divergence between UNN and UN. Some upward adjustment to UN may be needed to attain stability of the rate of inflation, but it will be small.

In addition, although UN is independent of demand-management policy, it is capable of being influenced by other government programmes. Frictional employment can be reduced by increasing the flow of labour market information and by lowering barriers to the occupational and geographical mobility of labour. 'Monetarist analysis suggests that it is the tools of high-employment policy, rather than its goals, that must be changed.'[110] Full employment can still be attained, not by demand-management policies but by labour market weapons to reduce UN.

Having evaluated the natural rate of unemployment for each EEC member, two problems still await resolution. First, as hinted earlier, a choice has to be made of a target inflation rate. This is no longer a long-run economic problem. Any inflation rate is compatible with each country's UN, and the decision on the appropriate target inflation rate is now purely political. Secondly, and more seriously, the problem of adjustment to each country's UN must be tackled. Not until that level is attained will the target inflation rate – or any other rate – become stable. The decision of a government over whether the costs of adjustment to UN are low enough to be counterbalanced by the gains of EMU will depend to a considerable extent on the discrepancy between current unemployment levels and UN. Sumner emphasises the costs of slow adjustment to a uniform or zero inflation rate and concludes that 'the immediate costs . . . will appear prohibitive to governments, in their concern for the short run.'[111] This, however, misses the main point – there may well be a short-run cost in a move from the current inflation rate to the target rate, but any permanent, long-run cost arises from an enforced movement from preferred unemployment levels to *UN*. The short-run costs should not be over-emphasised in the necessary adjustment to *UN*. The speed of adjustment to *UN* and the length of time chosen to introduce gradually a common currency area in Europe is a very rarely discussed topic. To quote Onida,

> . . . any choice of an 'optimal' solution makes no sense unless at the same time we understand what the 'optimum' path is which leads to that solution. Or else we fall into the temptation . . . of amusing ourselves with more or less refined descriptions of a world which we still do not now how to get to.[112]

A comparison of the natural rate of unemployment and the 1973 unemployment levels for each member depicts the adjustment problem admirably:[113]

	UN	*U* (1973)	% ΔU needed for *U* = *UN*
Belgium–Luxembourg	5·523	3·7	+49·3
Denmark	9·336	2·8	+233·4
France	0·194	2·14	*
Germany	2·091	1·2	+74·3
Ireland	6·973	7·2	−3·2
Italy	3·854	3·4	+13·4
Netherlands	6·760	3·0	+125·3
UK	2·071	4·1	*

A considerable increase in unemployment is needed for price stability in Belgium, Denmark, Germany and the Netherlands. This increase should be spread over a number of years – for example, a decade – with EMU being gradually introduced in and finally confirmed at the end of that period. Any attempt to introduce EMU over a very short time-period (e.g. two years) will probably cause the governments of these countries to doubt if the costs in terms of higher unemployment are worth incurring. These are not surprising conclusions. In recent years, all the economies – except Ireland – have been run at less than the natural level of unemployment and accelerating inflation has been experienced. However, the more stable inflation rates of 1958–69 were experienced at relatively low unemployment levels too, suggesting that most countries must have experienced an increase in *UN* in the 1970s. The reversal of that increase could be sought and if achieved could certainly help the adjustment needed for the introduction of a monetary union in Europe.

THE CHOICE OF AN EQUAL RATE OF INFLATION
The arguments in this section have been put forward under the assumption that in a fixed exchange rate or a common currency world, balance of payments disequilibria can be avoided in the long run by each country having the same inflation rate.[114] This view, based on the mechanism of excess monetary growth leading to inflation above the target rate and balance of payments deficit, which can only be corrected by cutting monetary growth to reduce inflation to its target rate, was criticised in Chapter 2. It is clear from that section that disequilibria can be cumulative due to differences in the reaction of demands to price and income changes, i.e. if elasticities differ among members equilibrium will not necessarily result.

To investigate the variability of income and price elasticities of demand for imports and exports in the EEC, a number of tests were carried out.

Import Elasticities
It was postulated that imports were determined by income and prices, with income entering contemporaneously and import prices lagged by one period. In addition, the import price variable was divided by the domestic retail price index to form a relative price variable.

The following equation was fitted for all EEC members:

$$\text{Log } M_t = \alpha + \beta \text{Log} Y_t + \delta \text{Log}(Pm/P)_{t-1} + \epsilon_t \qquad (29)$$

A logarithmic functional form was chosen as it exhibited a generally better fit than a linear form, while the coefficient β and δ are immediately interpretable as elasticities. The following elasticities were obtained:

	β (income elasticity)	δ (price elasticity)
Belgium–Luxembourg	1·22	−0·32
	(22·32)	(2·05)
Denmark	1·03	0·26
	(13·80)	(1·20)
France	1·30	0·28
	(16·07)	(0·83)
Germany	0·88	−0·69
	(10·33)	(2·49)
Ireland	1·06	−0·11
	(10·29)	(0·31)
Italy	1·21	−0·14
	(10·64)	(0·46)
Netherlands	0·96	−0·15
	(9·61)	(0·48)
UK	1·33	0·37
	(8·24)	(0·72)

The results show considerable stability and consistent values for the income elasticities. The range of values from 0·88 to 1·33 is not great, but sufficient to cause different responses to an equal change in national income. The price elasticities are less satisfactory and in general show the essential nature of many EEC imports with the elasticities being correctly signed and significant for Belgium and Germany only. Again, the range of values from −0·69 to 0·37 is not great.

Export Elasticities

To estimate a satisfactory equation for exports is less easy because of the problems of defining appropriate income and price variables. The following procedures were adopted.

Income variable. A weighted income variable was formed with all other EEC countries, and any other country contributing 2 per cent or more of a country's exports, included. The weights corresponding to the share of a country in the home country's exports were then corrected upwards to equal 100 per cent. The weights were multiplied by the relevant country's national income and then summed

$$Yw_j = \sum_{i=1}^{\Lambda} wi_t \, (Yi)_t/100 \tag{30}$$

where wi is the percentage contribution of the ith country $(i = 1 \ldots n)$ in the exports of country j.

Price variable. This was defined as $(Px/Pw)_j$ where

$$Pw_j = \sum_{i=1}^{\Lambda} wi_t \, (Yi)_t/100 \tag{31}$$

in this equation $Y_t = \alpha + \beta Yw + \delta(Px/Pw) + \epsilon_t$ (32)

Various lags were tried on both price and income variables and the following elasticities obtained:

	β (income elasticity)	δ (price elasticity)
Belgium–Luxembourg	$1\cdot40\ t - 1$	$-0\cdot30\ t - 1$
	$(6\cdot94)$	$(0\cdot57)$
Denmark	$8\cdot18\ t$	$-14\cdot61\ t - 2$
	$(0\cdot42)$	$(0\cdot94)$
France	$1\cdot46\ t - 1$	$-0\cdot42\ t - 3$
	$(23\cdot37)$	$(1\cdot19)$
Germany	$0\cdot60\ t - 1$	$-2\cdot45\ t - 1$
	$(1\cdot00)$	$(1\cdot77)$
Ireland	$3\cdot30\ t$	$-7\cdot33\ t - 3$
	$(2\cdot42)$	$(5\cdot94)$
Italy	$1\cdot34\ t - 1$	$-1\cdot16\ t - 1$
	$(13\cdot08)$	$(4\cdot09)$
Netherlands	$1\cdot46\ t - 1$	$1\cdot05\ t - 1$
	$(4\cdot89)$	$(0\cdot11)$
UK	$6\cdot48\ t$	$-9\cdot29\ t - 3$
	$(2\cdot18)$	$(4\cdot90)$

These results show that exports respond to price changes less quickly than they do to income changes. In addition, the export elasticities show much greater diversity than do those for imports.

To show how these different elasticities affect external

balance, the cases of Germany and Italy were investigated. The following assumptions were made:

(i) As in Chapter 2, each GDP is at $1000m., with exports and imports both equal to $100m. and in equilibrium at the start of the exercise.

(ii) A target rate of inflation (and therefore of export prices) of 5 per cent per annum was chosen.

(iii) The growth rate of real GDP (based on 1969–73 figures) was:

        Germany   5·9% p.a.
        Italy   4·9% p.a.

(iv) The rise in import prices was:

        Germany   4·9% p.a.
        Italy   3·7% p.a.

(v) The growth in export demand – based on the export income variable outlined above – was:

        Germany   4·3% p.a.
        Italy   6·1% p.a.

(vi) The appropriate elasticity values were taken from the earlier tables, i.e.

	Germany	Italy
Imports		
Income elasticity	0·88	1·21
Price elasticity	−0·69	−0·14
Exports		
Income elasticity	0·60	1·34
Price elasticity	−2·45	−1·16

A simulated exercise over three time-periods will show that within that period both Germany and Italy move into deficit on the external account:

Trade balance after three periods

	Exports ($m.)	Imports ($m.)	Balance ($m.)
Germany	73·78	105·54	−31·76
Italy	107·29	117·11	−9·82

Why has this happened?

Germany. Exports have fallen because the price elasticity of demand for them is very high, while the income elasticity which has a positive effect is much lower. Imports have risen for the opposite reason, because income elasticity is higher. The discrepancy is further exacerbated by a slower rate of growth of export demand (4·3 per cent) than import demand, i.e. GDP (5·9 per cent).

Italy. Both exports and imports have risen, due to a higher income elasticity of demand than price elasticity in both cases. Also, the rate of price change which affects imports and exports respectively is always less than the relevant rate of income change, such that the negative effect caused by higher prices is in both cases less than the positive effect caused by higher demand.

However, imports have risen faster than exports to put Italy in deficit, as the income elasticity of imports is much higher relative to the price elasticity than is the case for exports. This overwhelms the effect of higher exports due to a faster rate of growth of export demand (6·1 per cent) than domestic GDP (4·9 per cent).

In summary, *ceteris paribus*, imports (exports) rise faster the larger is the income elasticity of demand for imports (exports) and the faster the growth of GDP (and any other appropriate demand variable) and the smaller is the price elasticity of demand for imports (exports) and the lower the rate of import (domestic) price inflation.

Short of a complex programming exercise to calculate elasticities and rates of growth, etc., the implementation of a target rate of inflation will help remove intra-EEC disequilibria. However, it is clear from this section that such a policy does not tell the whole story. Differing responses to changing income and price levels could still place a country in disequilibrium with its partners despite an equal rate of inflation.

4 Summary and Conclusions

This book has been a study in the economic theory of currency areas, applied where relevant to the case-study of the European Economic Community. It has been of a special nature because of its analysis of the EEC in the light of currency area theory, with only passing reference to whether 'optimality' – in the strict economic sense described above – could be more nearly approached by expanding or reducing the membership of the Community. The study has made only limited reference to the non-economic, political and social arguments within the EEC, except to appraise why EMU is a priority for some members of the EEC. This concentration on economic theory and its empirical verification does not reduce its applicability to the arguments often quoted for and against EMU. It is an attempt to evaluate the conditions for a successful (i.e. where positive net benefits accrue), even if not an optimal, currency area in the EEC. It leaves the social and political arguments and decisions to those more capable of concluding on them.

Fleming[1] states that 'in any uniform exchange-rate area based on the EEC with its present (pre-1973), or with an expanded, membership it is difficult to escape the conclusion that the propensity to develop internal disequilibria and the difficulty of reconciling high employment with reasonable price stability would be even greater than in the United States.' He cites as major reasons for this the undoubted labour immobility, the low degree of wage and price flexibility, and the unlikelihood that a centralised fiscal authority will be introduced in the EEC. This is a pessimistic view, which this study vigorously opposes. Mundell's criterion based on factor mobility has been shown to be full of complications and even some confusion over the direction in which labour should flow – whether from high cost to low cost areas or vice versa? In practice, factor mobility – particularly with reference to labour – is very rarely perfect except in the tiniest geographical area, which is an irrelevance to currency area theory. Occupational differentials are major factors which are unlikely ever to be removed. As an equilibrating mechanism, factor mobility cannot be relied on in any one EEC country – let alone over the whole Community. While this will translate individual member regional problems to the Community level, the fear that widespread peripheral areas, e.g. the UK, southern Italy and Denmark, will become depressed is surely unlikely. A Community regional policy would be required when EMU is set up, a fact well appreciated by member governments, which will not be an inimical introduction as such policies exist in member states anyway. Clearly, Mundell's criterion is not being satisfied in any *one* EEC country – or many others in the world for that matter – and this is not a crucial argument against EMU, assuming a viable regional policy can be set up.

The criteria of McKinnon and Kenen are nearer to – or at least as near to – being satisfied on a Community-wide basis. Evidence presented earlier shows that the openness of the individual EEC economies is considerably greater in 1973 than it was in 1958. Assuming the theoretical doubts over the prescription of McKinnon's theory can be removed, the EEC is an eminently suitable currency area and will become more so through time if the trends of the nearly twenty years of EEC existence are continued.

The diversity of output of any one EEC country is clearly less than the diversity of output on the Community as a whole. This is not a surprising result as the combination of any group of countries into a monetary union will leave the number of individual goods produced at a higher level than in any individual of that union. Whether a greater percentage of total output will be concentrated on one product or group of products is more debatable, however. If so, one could say the currency area is less well diversified than some of its members. This is unlikely to be the case with the EEC. Many of the members have wide industrial bases, and the result of a monetary union should be a large, vibrant currency area with a highly diversified output. It is difficult to imagine a shift in demand or supply for any one commodity that would cause such disequilibria within the EEC as to force an individual country to alter its exchange rate. The oil crisis of 1973 is possibly one example. The balance of payments problems caused by that episode were severe because of the inelastic demand for oil imports. But, the external balance troubles were not unique to one or a number of the EEC countries – all members suffered, although some more than others. The need for intra-EEC parity changes was not great, and the devaluation of a 'European' currency – a perfectly feasible policy in an EEC currency area – would have been a sensible move. The fact that this traumatic episode would not invalidate the criteria Kenen for the EEC, and the fact that such a quadrupling of price plus an embargo is unlikely ever to be repeated for any commodity, suggests that the EEC satisfies Kenen's criterion admirably. This view is further justified if the British oil resources of the North Sea are to be as rich as expected. In that case, another OPEC oil price rise of the 1973 magnitude is unlikely, as all EEC countries would turn to Britain for their supplies. Intra-EEC disequilibria could spring up as a result, with Britain in heavy surplus – but this is unlikely, particularly if UK oil prices are no more expensive than the price of oil from the Middle East.

The relevance of these semi-automatic theories – although hardly discouraging for the project of EMU – has been played down because of the large role member governments could play in the attempt to make a monetary union successful. Evidence presented in Chapter 3 shows the undoubted presence of different trade-offs in member countries between unemployment and inflation in the short run both in terms of slope and position of the trade-off. These trade-offs cannot be expected to converge – they are independent of government demand-management policy, being determined by such structural factors as the friction in the labour market, the prevalence and strength of monopolies – both of commodity and labour supply, and the variability in demands and supplies for the goods produced in individual countries. These are the structural elements which Magnifico[2] emphasises and which clearly will only marginally converge if EMU is set up.

This would have been, in our opinion, a savage blow to the prospects for EMU but for the unearthing of the overwhelming evidence that a trade-off between unemployment and inflation does not exist in the long run. There is only doubt on this proposition for France and Belgium, and if this uncertainty could be removed for these two countries this would be a clinching argument in favour of EMU. As it is, the argument is very strong and probably decisive. The only economic problem that remains is to move the economies of the EEC towards their natural rate of unemployment in such a way that the adjustment costs in terms, perhaps, of labour unrest are spread over a long period. The political problem then remains of the choice of a uniform inflation rate – perhaps it should be zero[3] – and the institution of a common monetary policy to achieve that goal. If this movement is successful with individual governments being able to maintain accurately the economy at the natural level of unemployment and the target inflation rate, the result traditionally will be balance of payments equilibrium for all members. It has been suggested in Chapters 2 and 3 that despite the fulfilment of all the above conditions, balance of payments disequilibria may still spring up because of differential rates of growth of real output, and different income and price elasticities of demand for imports and exports. If such a situation arises, there are three alternatives. First, an attempt can be made empirically to evaluate the necessary rates of price inflation to achieve external balance for each member. Secondly, a scheme could be set up to subsidise those countries in deficit from the external surpluses of other members. If either of these two conditions could be met, exchange rates could be gradually locked over the adjustment period and then, when the time is opportune, individual currencies withdrawn and a European currency introduced. A third alternative would be to abandon the attempt to establish a European currency area, which in our opinion would be an unwarranted reaction, as so many of the preconditions of a successful union in the EEC exist.

Obviously, when and if the time becomes ripe and the members are willing to introduce a common currency, the project itself will have taken on more significance than a simple fixed exchange system. A common currency implies the introduction of a Community monetary policy with the removal of any national control on monetary and banking affairs. It also means a considerably greater degree of capital market integration than exists at present and the introduction of a widely acceptable low risk Community security in which the authorities can undertake open market operations for the purposes of monetary control. These two features, which are essential to EMU, represent considerable loss of national sovereignty for every member country and are the political barriers which must be cleared – and they may be more difficult to do so than are the economic barriers discussed earlier – before an EMU can become operational.

Two further developments are necessary, however, for EMU. First, while the harmonisation to a degree of taxation systems is necessary – and in fact already exists in large part, e.g. the recent introduction of Value Added Tax in the UK – the development of a Community fiscal authority on the lines of the monetary authority mentioned above, is not necessary. Secondly, there is no need for the much feared introduction of a European nation–state to occur. Political unity is not a necessary condition for EMU, although the reverse is the case. The authors in this book are not arguing for political union, and they are not stating that the political, social and human conditions for unification exist in the EEC. All they have set out to do is to evaluate the EEC as a currency area from an economist's viewpoint – untainted, we hope, by value judgements. It is the argument of this book that from an economic angle, EMU is conceivable and will work. To put the matter another way, if the only doubt remaining in a movement towards political union in the EEC was the economic justification for it, this book has set out to clinch that case. The EEC may not be an 'optimal' currency area, but it is likely to be a successful one.

Notes

CHAPTER 1

1. 'Report to the Council and the Commission on the Realisation by stages of Economic and Monetary Union in the Community', *The Werner Report*, bulletin 11 (1970).
2. Ibid., p. 10.
3. Ibid., p. 12.
4. Commission of the European Communities, Com (73) 570 (Apr 1973) p. 8.
5. Source: EEC Statistical Office, 1973 figures.

CHAPTER 2

1. J. E. Meade, 'The Balance of Payments problems of EFTA', *Economic Journal* vol. 67 (Sep 1957) pp. 376–96 and *Economic Theory and Western European Integration*, T. Scitovsky, London Union, 1958.
2. R. A. Mundell, 'A Theory of Optimal Currency Areas', *American Economic Review* (Sep 1961) pp. 657–65.
3. R. I. McKinnon, 'Optimal Currency Areas', *American Economic Review* (Sep 1963) pp. 717–24.
4. P. B. Kenen, 'The Theory of Optimal Currency Areas: an eclectic view', *in Monetary Problems of the International Economy,* ed. A. Swobada and R. A. Mundell (Chicago, 1969) pp. 41–60.
5. Op. cit., p. 657.
6. J. M. Fleming, 'On Exchange Rate Unification', *Economic Journal* (Sep 1971).
7. G. Magnifico, 'European Monetary Unification for Balanced Growth: A New Approach', *Essays in International Finance,* no. 88 (Princeton, N. J., Aug 1971).
8. G. E. Wood, 'European Monetary Union and the UK – A cost-benefit analysis', *Surrey Papers in Economics,* no. 9 (July 1973).
9. See, for example, an otherwise excellent summary article, A. Reitsma, 'Currency Areas and All that', *Bankers' Magazine* (Mar 1972).
10. H. G. Johnson, 'Conditions of International Monetary Equilibrium: Equilibrium under Fixed exchange rates', *American Economic Review* (May 1963).
11. Op. cit., pp. 659–60.
12. Op. cit., p. 663.

13. A simple example can show this:

ULC (unit labour costs) $= \dfrac{W}{Q/L}$

where W = real wages
Q/L ≤ output per man (productivity)

Area	W	Q/L	ULC
A	100	10	10
B	40	2	20

A is the high wage area B the high ULC area.

14. For a discussion of this point see J. M. Fleming, 'On Exchange Rate Unification', *Economic Journal* (Sep 1971) pp. 472–4.
15. E. Heckscher, 'The effects of foreign trade on the distribution of income', *Ekonomiks Tidskrift* (1919), reprinted in *Readings in the theory of international trade,* ed. H. Ellis and A. Metzler (Philadelphia, 1949).
16. Op. cit., p. 659.
17. Op. cit., p. 717.
18. See, for example, F. Machlup, 'In Search of Guides for Policy', in *Maintaining and Restoring Balance in International Payments,* W. Fellner *et al.* (Princeton, N. J., 1966).
19. Op. cit., p. 663.
20. W. M. Corden 'Monetary Integration' *Essays in International France,* No. 93 (Princeton, N.J., Apr 1972).
21. Op. cit., p. 49.
22. Ibid.
23. Ibid.
24. G. E. Wood, 'European Monetary Union and the U.K. – A Cost-Benefit Analysis', *Surrey Papers in Economics* no. 9 (1973).
25. For a further elaboration of this section see Fellner *et al.*, *Maintaining and Restoring Balance in International Payments,* (Princeton, N. J. 1966) chapters by Fellner, Triffin and Machlup.
26. R. I. McKinnon and W. Oates, 'The Implications of International Economic Integration for Monetary, Fiscal and Exchange Rate Policy', *Studies in International Finance,* no. 16 (Princeton N. J. 1966).
27. R. A. Mundell, 'Capital Mobility and Stabilisation Policy under Fixed and Flexible Exchange Rates', *Canadian Journal of Economics and Science,* XXIX (Nov 1963).
28. 'Monetarist' here refers to that view of monetary union put forward in particular by France and the European Commission in Brussels; it must not be confused with monetarism and the Chicago School of Thought in Economics.
29. For an expansion of this point see J. R. Presley and P. Coffey, 'On Exchange Rate Unification – A Comment in relation to the EEC, *Economic Journal* (Sep 1972), and P. Coffey and J. Presley, *European Monetary Integration* (London, 1971).
30. See, as a starting point, R. Musgrave, *The Theory of Public Finance,* (McGraw-Hill, 1959).

31. J. Tinbergen, *On the Theory of Economic Policy* (Amsterdam, 1952).
32. The curve takes its name from A. W. Phillips, who wrote 'The Relation between the Rate of change in Money, Wage Rates and Unemployment in the United Kingdom 1861–1957', *Economica*, xxv (Nov 1958) pp. 283–99.
33. Op. cit., p. 476.
34. Op. cit., pp. 11–14.
35. Op. cit., p. 75.
36. E.g. a 10 per cent increase in output per man will counteract a 10 per cent rise in money wage rates, leaving unit labour costs unchanged.
37. M. T. Sumner, 'European Monetary Union and the Control of Europe's Inflation Rate', *University of Manchester Discussion Paper* (July 1974) p. 14.
38. Ibid.
39. See, for example, J. M. Parkin, 'The Causes of Inflation: recent contributions and current controversies', University of Manchester, Inflation Workshop Discussion Paper 7405 (1974).
40. Op. cit., p. 12.
41. A. G. Hines, 'Trade Unions and Wage Inflation in the U.K. 1893–1961', *Review of Economic Studies* (1964).
42. M. Friedman, 'The Role of Monetary Policy', *American Economic Review* (Mar 1968). E. S. Phelps, 'Money Wage Dynamics and Labour Market Equilibrium', *Journal of Political Economy* (1968).
43. M. Friedman and D. Laidler, 'Unemployment versus Inflation: An Evaluation of the Phillips Curve', *Institute of Economic Affairs*, lecture no. 2 (June 1975).
44. J. M. Parkin, 'An Overwhelming Case for European Monetary Union', *Banker* (Sep 1972).
45. Income elasticity $= \dfrac{\text{per cent change in demand for imports}}{\text{per cent change in income}}$

   Price elasticity $= \dfrac{\text{per cent change in demand for imports}}{\text{per cent change in price level}}$

CHAPTER 3

1. F. Onida, 'The theory and policy of optimal currency areas and their implications for European Monetary Union', SUERF series, 9A (1972), p. 30.
2. A. J. Reitsma, 'Currency Areas and All That', *Bankers' Magazine* (Mar 1972) p. 108.
3. H. G. Johnson, 'Problems of European Monetary Union', *Euromoney* (Apr 1971).
4. Op. cit.
5. Mundell, in fact, stated that factor mobility is necessary for internal balance if wages and prices are inflexible. Flexibility of wages and prices, if in existence, can take the place of exchange rate changes in achieving internal balance. Clearly, there is substantial wage and price stickiness – particularly downwards – in the EEC.
6. Op. cit.

7. Wood (1973) doubts the existence of any substantial labour mobility even in the UK, saying that on Mundell's criterion 'the U.K. currency area is already too large'.

8. P. Jay, 'Conditions for a Common European Currency', *International Currency Review* (Jan 1970).

9. Op. cit.

10. M. Boleat, 'Integration and harmonisation in Europe', *National Westminster Bank Review* (May 1975).

11. Op. cit.

12. W. G. Minot, 'Tests for Integration between Major Western European Capital Markets', *Oxford Economic Papers* (Nov 1974).

13. Op. cit.

14. R. Triffin, in 'The Community and the Disruption of the World Monetary System', *Banca Nazionale del Lavoro Review* (1975), notes that the bonds placed on the Eurodollar market have grown from $9 million in 1964 to $185 million in 1974.

15. Op. cit.

16. Op. cit.

17. This is similar to the argument of Johnson cited earlier in relation to the CAP.

18. Such a study is not simply begging the question as to whether the McKinnon assumption is more valid than the alternative one put forward by Corden. If it could be established whether the EEC exhibited a fairly uniform degree of 'openness' the appropriate conclusion in the fixed *v.* flexible rates debate would follow an analysis of the origin of most disturbances to domestic prices.

19. R. B. Cross and D. E. W. Laidler, 'Inflation, Excess Demand and Expectations in Fixed Exchange-Rate Open Economies: Some preliminary empirical results', *University of Manchester Inflation Workshop Discussion Papers,* no. 7410 (Manchester, 1974).

20. 'The distinction between tradables and non-tradables has usually been regarded as a piece of analytic fiction that enables certain theoretical notions to be expressed with simplicity rather than as a serious operational classification of the goods that enter into national income.' Cross and Laidler, op. cit., p. 5.

21. B. Balassa, 'Monetary Integration in the European Common Market', in A. K. Swoboda (ed.), *Europe and the Evolution of the International Monetary System* (London 1973).

22. All data in this study – except where otherwise stated – is annual, covering the period from 1958 to 1973. 1958 is a convenient starting date, being the first year of operation of the EEC. Individual data was not always available for Luxembourg, and in those cases the data for Belgium and Luxembourg is combined.

23. J. Johnston, *Econometric Methods* (New York, 1972) p. 344.

24. When the Two Stage Least-Squares estimates of β are compared to the APM, a significant difference between them is noticed for Belgium, again, and also the UK (at a 10 per cent significance level).

25. Op. cit., p. 721.

26. Op. cit.
27. Op cit.
28. Denmark provided results that appeared to make it as closed as the USA; the authors suggested that the use of index-linked wage rate setting may have caused such an anomalous result.
29. Reitsma, Op. cit.; D. Robertson, 'Is there a case for European Monetary Union?', *Bankers' Magazine* (Mar 1972).
30. Op. cit.
31. J. C. Ingram, 'Comment: The Currency Area Problems', in R. A. Mundell and A. K. Swoboda (eds), *Monetary Problems of the International Economy* (Chicago, 1969).
32. Op. cit.
33. Op. cit., p. 107.
34. Op. cit., p. 108.
35. Op. cit., p. 9.
36. The data came from the UN *Yearbook of National Accounts,* Section 2. Separate data was available for Luxembourg for this test.
37. The eleven sectors for 1971 were:
    1. Agriculture, Hunting, Forestry and Fishing.
    2. Mining and Quarrying.
    3. Manufacturing.
    4. Construction.
    5. Electricity, Gas and Water.
    6. Transport, Storage and Communication.
    7. Wholesale and Retail Trade, Restaurants and Hotels.
    8. Finance, Insurance, Real Estate and Business Services.
    9. Ownership of dwellings.
    10. Public Administration and Defence.
    11. Services.
38. See, for example, H. G. Johnson, 'Inflation: a monetarist view', in *Further Essays in Monetary Economics* (London, 1972).
39. Wood, op. cit., p. 10.
40. Balassa, op. cit., p. 111.
41. G. Magnifico, *European Monetary Unification* (London, 1973) Chapter 2.
42. Hines, op. cit.
43. D. Purdy and G. Zis, 'Trade Unions and Wage Inflation in the U.K.: A Reappraisal', in D. E. W. Laidler and D. Purdy (eds), *Inflation and Labour Markets* (Manchester, 1974).
44. R. Ward and G. Zis, 'Trade Union Militancy as an Explanation of Inflation. An International Comparison', *Manchester School* (Mar 1974).
45. See, for example, J. M. Parkin, 'An Overwhelming Case for EMU', *Banker* (Sep 1972).
46. J. M. Parkin, 'European and World Money', *Banker* (Jan 1973).
47. Op. cit.
48. There is less evidence for the existence of such a trade-off in the long run. See pp. 69–88 below.

49. Op. cit.
50. Op. cit., p. 20.
51. E.g. R. G. Lipsey, 'The relation between unemployment and the rate of change of money wage rates in the United Kingdom, 1862–1957: A further analysis', *Economica* (1960), and L. R. Klein and R. G. Bodkin, 'Empirical Aspects of the Trade-Off among Three Goals: High Level Employment, Price Stability and Economic Growth', in *Inflation, Growth and Employment* (Englewood Cliffs, N. J., 1964).
52. J. M. Parkin, M. T. Sumner and R. Ward, 'The Effects of Excess Demand, Generalised Expectations and Wage Price Controls on Wage Inflation in the U.K.' *University of Manchester Inflation Workshop Discussion Paper,* no. 7402 (Manchester, 1974).
53. N. Duck, J. M. Parkin, D. Rose and G. Zis, 'The Determination of the Rate of Change of Wages and Prices in the Fixed Exchange-rate World Economy', *University of Manchester Inflation Workshop Discussion Paper,* no. 7404 (Manchester 1974).
54. W. D. Nordhaus, 'The World-Wide Wages Explosion', *Brookings Papers on Economic Activity,* no. 2 (1972).
55. D. E. W. Laidler and B. Corry, 'Some Empirical Tests of Phillips' Relationship' mimeo. (London School of Economics, 1967).
56. Where $\dot{w}t$ = rate of change of money wage-rates and U_t = unemployment.
57. To test the hypothesis that the Phillips' curve was stable until recent years, the data was split at 1967 and the following values for β obtained:

	1958–67	1968–73
Belgium–Luxembourg	−1·909	−2·466
Denmark	−1·020	−1·440
France	−4·657	1·014
Germany	−1·192	−10·185
Ireland	−1·303	2·666
Italy	−2·504	−25·274
Netherlands	−5·016	1·273
UK	−2·652	3·325

The argument for EMU based on similar trade-offs between inflation and unemployment was more persuasive before 1968 than it is today! The resultant rate of unemployment for each country at the target level of wage inflation of 5 per cent was:

	1958–67	1968–73
Belgium–Luxembourg	4·381	5·772
Denmark	8·182	10·053
France	1·838	−4·344
Germany	2·716	1·488
Ireland	8·035	3·520
Italy	4·786	3·719
Netherlands	1·821	−2·679
UK	1·752	1·414

58. Balassa, op. cit., p. 104.
59. Parkin op. cit. (Sep 1972) p. 1142.
60. Op. cit., p. 20.
61. M. T. Sumner, 'European Monetary Integration and the Control of Europe's Inflation Rate', *University of Manchester Inflation Workshop Discussion Paper,* no. 7411 (Manchester, 1974) p. 10.
62. M. Friedman, 'The Role of Monetary Policy', *American Economic Review* (1968), and E. S. Phelps, 'Phillips Curves, Expectations of Inflation and Optimal Unemployment over time', *Economica* (Aug 1967).
63. A method has recently been suggested in J. A. Carlson and J. M. Parkin, 'Inflation Expectations', *Economica* (May 1975), for converting such qualitative data into a series for $\dot{p}^e$.
64. Op. cit. Results for non-EEC countries are not reviewed here but can be found in J. M. Parkin, 'The Causes of Inflation: Recent Contributions and Current Controversy', *University of Manchester Inflation Workshop Discussion Paper,* no. 7405, (Manchester 1974), and in D. E. W. Laidler and J. M. Parkin, 'Inflation: A Survey', *Economic Journal* (Dec 1975).
65. Parkin, Sumner and Ward, op. cit.
66. R. G. Lipsey and J. M. Parkin, 'Incomes Policy: A Reappraisal', *Economica* (1970).
67. F. Modigliani and E. Tarantelli, 'A Generalisation of the Phillips' Curve for a Developing Country', *Review of Economic Studies* (Oct 1973).
68. The alternative functional form of $\frac{1}{U_t}$ was tried, but found to be, on balance, inferior. $\dot{P}_t$ equals rate of change of prices with superscript e referring to expectations.
69. Op. cit.
70. 'Inflation: the Present Problem', OECD, (Paris, 1970).
71. F. P. R. Brechling, 'Some Empirical Evidence on the Effectiveness of Prices and Incomes Policies', in J. M. Parkin and M. T. Sumner (eds), *Incomes Policy and Inflation* (Manchester, 1972).
72. Op. cit.
73. L. M. Koyck, *Distributed Lags and Investment Analysis* (Amsterdam, 1954).
74. J. A. Carlson and J. M. Parkin, op. cit.
75. D. Rose, 'A general error–learning model of expectations formation', *University of Manchester Inflation Workshop Discussion Paper,* no. 7210 (Manchester, 1972).
76. T. J. Sargent, 'A Note on the Accelerationist Controversy', *Journal of Money, Credit and Banking* (1971).
77. Friedman and Laidler, op. cit.
78. G. O. Bierwag and M. A. Grove, 'Aggregate Koyck Functions', *Econometrica* (1966).
79. P. G. Saunders and A. R. Nobay, 'Price Expectations, the Phillips' Curve and Incomes Policy', in Parkin and Sumner, op. cit.
80. Op. cit.

81. J. M. Parkin, 'Incomes Policy: some further results on the rate of change of money wages', *Economica* (1970).
82. Op. cit.
83. Op. cit.
84. The equations for France, West Germany and the Netherlands are not, however, well behaved in all respects, casting some doubt on this conclusion for these countries.
85. S. J. Turnovsky, in 'The Expectations Hypothesis and the Aggregate Wage Equation: Some Empirical Evidence for Canada', *Economica* (Feb 1972), used a similar procedure for Canada.
86. Op. cit.
87. Turnovsky, op. cit.
88. However, the adjustment parameter (f) for Germany is greater than one, which is an unusual result.
89. Y^T was calculated by fitting the regression $Y = f(t)$ for all EEC countries.
90. G. W. Smith, 'Excess Demand and Expectations as Determinants of Price Changes in the United Kingdom Manufacturing Sector', *University of Manchester Inflation Workshop Discussion Paper*, no. 7505 (Manchester, 1975).
91. A. Knöbl, 'Price Expectations and Actual Price Behaviour in Germany', *IMF Staff Papers* (Mar 1974).
92. Op. cit.
93. Other formulations of excess demand were used – including the use of Gross National Product and the calculation of a more complex trend – but the results in Table 3.13 were superior to all these alternatives.
94. R. M. Solow, *Price Expectations and the Behaviour of the Price Level* (Manchester, 1969).
95. Op. cit.
96. Op. cit.
97. Op. cit. (1975).
98. Op. cit.
99. Op. cit.
100. A recent paper by J. M. Parkin and G. W. Smith, 'Inflationary Expectations and the long-run trade-off between inflation and unemployment in open economies', *University of Manchester Inflation Workshop Discussion Paper*, no. 7509 (Manchester, 1975), shows that using retail prices as a proxy for price expectations may result, in a fixed exchange rate, open economy, in an estimate of the expectations coefficient which is below unity but biased. Given the undoubted openness of many EEC economies and the adjustable peg quasi-fixed rate regime of the 1950s and 1960s, any future doubts on the values of the expectations coefficients of around 0·6–0·8 are removed. The 'no long-run trade-off' hypothesis is clearly vindicated in nearly all cases.
101. Friedman, op. cit. (1968).
102. Friedman and Laidler, op. cit.

103. Op. cit.
104. Op. cit., p. 31
105. J. Tobin, 'Inflation and Unemployment', *American Economic Review* (Mar 1972).
106. A productivity index (for 1958–73) was available for all EEC countries from the *Yearbook of Labour Statistics* (ILO). Productivity was defined for France as final gross production per man-hour, and for all other countries as GNP per employed person.
107. Some of the discrepancies may be due to different methods of measuring unemployment.
108. Tobin, op. cit.
109. M. R. Gray and R. G. Lipsey, 'Is the natural rate of unemployment the appropriate policy target for maintaining a stable rate of inflation?', *University of Manchester Discussion Paper*, no. 7408, (Manchester, 1974).
110. Laidler, op. cit. (1975) p. 47.
111. Op. cit., p. 18.
112. Op. cit., p. 25
113. The percentage change in unemployment needed is omitted for France and the UK due to the previously expressed doubts on the estimated values of *UN* for these countries.
114. See, for example, H. G. Johnson, 'Inflation: A Monetarist View', in *Further Essays in Monetary Economics* (London, 1973).

CHAPTER 4
1. Op. cit., p. 485
2. Op. cit. (1971).
3. Sumner, op. cit.

Index

illusion, money, 21
importables, 18
International Monetary Fund, 46
Ireland, 5, 52 *passim*
IS/LM curves, 43, 44
Italy, 4, 5, 48 *passim*, 99

Johnson, H. G., 10, 46

Kenen, P. B., 9, 12, 23 *passim*, 47, 60 *passim*, 99
Knöbl, A., 81

Laidler, D., 50, 54, 66, 77, 82, 84
Lipsey, R. G., 72, 90, 91
liquidity, 2

Magnifico, G., 10, 30, 33, 36, 101
Marjolin Report, 5
McKinnon, R. I., 9, 17 *passim*, 25, 28, 47, 60 *passim*, 99
Meade, J. E., 9, 47
mobility, factor, 12 *passim*, 47 *passim*, 99
Modigliani, F., 72
'monetarist', 3, 29, 37 *passim*, 91
multiplier, 13, 15
Mundell, R. A., 9, 10, 13 *passim*, 47, 60 *passim*, 98, 99

Netherlands, 4, 49 *passim*
Nobay, A. R., 77
Nordhaus, W. D., 66, 74

Oates, W., 28
Ohlin, B., 17
Onida, F., 66, 69, 92
Openness, 17–23, 50–60
Optimality (definition of), 9, 12, 17

Parkin, M., 38, 65, 69, 71 *passim*
Payments, balance of, 3 *passim*, 9, 10, 15, 34 *passim*
Phelps, E. S., 37, 69, 70, 72
Phillips' Curve, 30 *passim*
long run, 37, 66, 68, 69 *passim*

policy
expenditure reducing, 27, 28
expenditure switching, 27, 28
fiscal, 12, 23, 26, 29, 30
mix, 26, 29
monetary, 2, 12, 23, 26, 29, 30
Poll, Gallup, 71
Propensity to inflation, 30, 65

region, economic, 10
regional policy, 16, 29
Reitsma, A., 60
returns to scale, 15
Rose, D., 76

Sargent, T. J., 77
Saunders, P. G., 77
Schiller, Plan, 3
Scitovsky, T., 9, 48, 49
Smith, G. W., 81
Solow, R. M., 82
Sumner, M. T., 35, 71, 72, 89, 91

Tarantelli, E., 72
taxation, 2, 6, 7
theory, automatic adjustment, 11, 20, 47
Tinbergen, J., 30
Tobin, J., 89
trade-off, 32 *passim*, 63 *passim*
trading, bilateral, 11
transformation, Koyck, 76
Turkey, 48

U.K., 52 *passim*
Unemployment, natural level, 38, 70, 88, *passim*
Unions, trade, 21, 25, 65
Unit of account, 19
Unity political, 45
U.S.A., 54, 59, 61

Valuation, costs of, 11
Value-added tax, 6, 102

Ward, R., 65, 71, 72, 89
War, Vietnam, 46
Werner Report, 1,
Wood, G. E., 10, 26, 66

Yugoslavia, 48

Zis, G., 65